The Strand

Mike Russell

The Strand

Copyright © 2024 by Mike Russell

All rights reserved. No part of this book may be used or reproduced by any means, graphic, electronic, or mechanical, including photocopying, recording, taping, or by any information storage retrieval system without the written permission of the publisher except in the case of brief quotations embodied in critical articles and reviews.

ISBN: 979-8-9868130-3-5
Library of Congress Control Number: 9798986813035

Some poems by Mike Russell

Sacred Life Publishers™
SacredLife.com
Printed in the United States of America

Contents

Dedication v
The Strand vii
Introduction xi
Poem - Beautiful Willamette xvii
1 - The Introductions 1
    Queen City of the Trails 10
2 - The Journey Begins 13
    Poem - The Fog 19
3 - Traveling Back into Time 21
4 - The Reality 29
    Immigrant Wagons 35
5 - Truly into The West 39
    What Could Happen? 48
6 - The National Celebration 51
    If It Won't Kill You, It Will Make You Stronger 57
7 - The Depths of Grief 61
    Poem - The Understanding 68
8 - Destinies Fork in The Road 69
9 - The Trail Markers to Fort Hall 77
10 - The Hidden Secrets in Water 81
    Understanding Time 88
11 - The Union of Minds 91

12 - Trail Romances	99
Poem – The Least of the Expectations	104
13 - Whatever it Takes	105
14 - Holding onto Faith	115
15 - The Realization of What is Coming	119
16 - Facing the Odds with Determination	125
17 - The Meeting of a Giant	129
18 - Out of the Darkness	133
Poem - Against All Odds	137
19 - The Future is Understood	139
20 - Stepping into the Unknown	145
I'll Never Find Another You by The Seekers	148
Lansford W. Hasting-The Emigrants' Guide to Oregon and California - 1846	149
Closing Thoughts of the Future	151
Chief Joseph Quote	153
About the Author	155

Dedication

This book is the result of my deep interest in understanding the past and results from my search for myself within the fascinating world of Spirit and the connections through the thin veils of energy. It is easy to turn one's mind away from something that sounds like it could not happen. But, having spent years studying and trying to understand the connections between the past, present, and future in their relationship to life, I believe there is a solid connection to what some call the "Cycle of Life." I don't know anyone who can guarantee that there is only one way of viewing things, so I believe that I have lived before and will live again and that the people I meet in one lifetime are probably the same ones I hang out with in other lifetimes—so, having said that I want to dedicate this book to all those adventurous Spirits who hold onto the possibilities that there is more to life than being born and dying. You are a force in many possibilities, and I encourage you to keep searching.

Also, I would like to dedicate this book to those who journeyed on the Oregon Trail. Your dreams of going to a new land and improving your lives are commendable. Four to five months on the trail while enduring the daily hardships to get to a better place required dreaming, tenacity, persistence, and, in some ways, naivete. Without those, no one would have made it. Those who died on the Oregon Trail still left their marks one way or the other. The families that came and survived to this day through the generations can still be proud of the strength it took for the pioneers to reach out and help guide them.

Whether you are interested in history, human achievement stories, or a need to understand where you fit into the wheel of life, you are perfectly aligned to be here now and challenge your mind as you read these pages. Thank you for being part of this journey.

Finally, I would like to dedicate this book to my wife, Trisha Michael. Throughout our time together, she has been a trustworthy source of support and understanding that we all have unknown skills that, if given half a chance, can come out in surprising ways that meet our needs for purpose. As humans, we strive for purpose, but often, it is not shown to us or supported. Trisha has loved me without exception and supported me steadfastly on my writing journey.

The Strand

Understanding the threat of endless connections through the family's history is like following a cottonwood fluff floating through the air. You try to reach out for it, and it moves away. It floats in the air, weaving in and out of obstacles, hoping to find a place to land and spread its seed. This thread or strand connects everything in the past to everything in the future with an unseen force of place, time, and energy. You think you have a grasp of the historical facts, but you find out there is so much more to the story that you need help understanding.

Understanding nothing and feeling it all allows everyone to reflect on their histories and the fight to suppress wrongs while at the same time relishing the eye-opening adventures of the past. The strand runs through all the generations that have passed before us, and sometimes, that thread can spark a thought or a whole storyline. Understanding this connection is only part of it. Within the connection are many forgotten stories that we must dig up so they can reach the light of day. Without true stories, we are subjugated by myths, folklore, and made-up or ill-conceived thoughts about what may or may not have happened.

Digging into the depths of remembrances and holding

onto the words of those in the stories brings reflections that can hold onto and bring the characters, fictitious or real, to life. Time changes stories so much that no one knows what was real or made up.

The strand of energy that floats through the Oregon Trail stories connects those immigrants who traveled to the West Coast. Their hardships, work ethic, strength of will, and, yes, their deaths continue through the threads that connect to relatives. Some families can connect their stories to those who set out on an adventure, not knowing what was ahead but hoping their lives would improve. Everyone had a different story to tell. But they were all reaching for something better. The strand carries through all these stories in a way of connection. It weaves in and out of generations through DNA or the similarities of those who dared to think they had an answer for the problems of those times.

Many became successful, and many couldn't make it through. Yes, this is a repetitive story of all histories through the migratory movement of people. Humans love to stretch the boundaries of their realities in hoping the grass is greener somewhere else. Sometimes, they are, and sometimes humans discover it wasn't what they thought. Although we may never know whether the immigrants achieved what they had hoped, we do know from their writings what they went through to get to the promised land.

That may be the point. It is not necessarily the reason behind the moves we make as humans but the adventure of getting there. There will always be another Oregon Trail to entice us to go somewhere else, which is perfect. Knowing the strand is there, and we can notice connections to the past and future, can give us the foundation to challenge the concepts that hold us back from risking the adventure. Going into our futures knowing that this connection links us to our ancestors creates an understanding that we, too, can venture beyond our comfort zones. If we make it to the end of the journey, the strand going forward will carry our adventures to another generation to challenge their understanding of who they are. The cycle continues.

Introduction

Many times, as a child, while watching the Westerns of our time, of which there were many, I was caught between the worlds of make-believe and reality. I knew that television and movies were make-believe, but somewhere in me, there was a twinge of remembrance. I often wondered how people came West to establish homes and towns, and I had genuine compassion for the Native Americans and animals like the horses and buffalo. I did not understand as a child how we could have created such a diverse country from East to West while treating people so poorly. It made me sad, and at the same time, I wanted to do something. Of course, a child figures out quickly that time moves forward, and new experiences come along to take up those feelings or replace them with new experiences.

Luckily, I had a grandmother who was a Western artist who allowed me to live in a world where Native Americans had dignity. Her art, which now surrounds me, helped me to understand that not all stories of the West required the obliteration of a way of life. Her art contained majestic people and places in the West that ultimately created a love for the environment, nature, and the people that came before us.

Growing up in Arizona, although harsh at times, was a

perfect place to spend time in her thoughtful way of seeing things. It gave me a natural environment to see and feel the West. With its deserts and sunsets of multiple hues, I enjoyed camping and fishing. As many outdoor activities as I could work in among the standard daily living requirements, I could hold onto those long-ago inklings of what memories were triggered by seeing those movies and television shows.

My interest in the Oregon Trail was always in the back of my mind and was strengthened when my wife and I decided to move to Oregon in the 1970s. Over the many years I have lived in Oregon, my travels around the state have allowed me to cross paths with the trail. It was not until I lost my first wife and went inside searching for meaning in my life that I realized I still had the interests of that child who was so young.

So, over many years of trying to figure out who I am and want to be for the rest of my journey on this planet, I made a profound discovery that I could write. Through a series of different growth experiences in self and writing, all the experiences in my life that I thought were coincidental were indeed part of the journey. Although I did not know it then, they were all steppingstones going somewhere and ultimately meant something to me.

And so, the circle has been completed. I can write about

the Oregon Trail that I found so fascinating as a child, along with the people, the ups and downs of the unbelievable quest that the pioneers subjected themselves to in the hopes of reaching a land where they could improve the lives they wanted.

All their stories investigate their different values, mores, religions, and ethnic differences. The sometimes-naïve approach they had to take was terrific, as the hardships made many underestimate what they had to endure to get to the promised land. The publications of the times often were misleading. Sometimes, outright made-up stories of how easy it was and created a pot of gold at the end of the rainbow that was, in a way, grabbed up by those going because they needed to hold onto something that would allow them to leave a known world and go into the wilds. Otherwise, like all new explorations, no one would ever leave the safety of the known.

And so, thousands journeyed West, hoping that they and their families would prosper and benefit. Their stories are sometimes hard to read, and at other times, there can be so much joy in the little things that happen along the way. Death was said to occur every mile along the Oregon Trail, but they continued to come. Love and hate, accidents, births, and deaths just as today happened continuously, and if a family made it without losing anyone, it was indeed a miracle.

But what they achieved, as miraculous as it was, was just the tip of the iceberg. They created a new country, so to speak, as the British gave up territory and states were formed. Families grew, and towns were established all over the West. And to this day, there is a lot of history in the little towns along the Oregon Trail. The expansion of the West created the country that we know today. Manifest Destiny, the establishment of the railroads, and the displacement of the Indians all had negative and positive consequences.

The child in me is pained by the things that the young country accepted in the name of progress. Although I cannot excuse the past, I can take that as a human response and understand that history has a way of repeating man's inadequacies.

Throughout history, the story of advancing in the name of man has continued to impact people and places, and I can only hope that each generation will realize that there are more ways to march into the future that consider other people's views and that there is a balance to being part of the oneness of humanity.

This book has provided me with a way to marry the idea of multiple lives, history, and the feelings of a young child with compassion and a love of history and nature. The child's innocence dwells in this story, and I hope that the journey contained within sparks your interest.

BEAUTIFUL WILLAMETTE

Samuel L Simpson - Oregon Poet

From the Cascades' frozen gorges,
Leaping like a child at play,
Winding, widening through the valley,
Bright Willamette glides away;
Onward ever,
Lovely river,
Softly calling to the sea,
Time, that scars us,
Maims and mars us,
Leaves no track or trench of thee.

Spring's green witchery is weaving
Braid and border for thy side;
Grace forever haunts thy journey,
Beauty dimples on thy tide;
Through the purple gates of morning
Now thy roseate ripples dance,
Golden then, when day, departing,
On thy waters trails his lance.
Waltzing, flashing,
Tinkling, splashing,

Limpid, volatile, and free —
Always hurried
To be buried
In the bitter, moon-mad sea.

In thy crystal deeps inverted
Swings a picture of the sky,
Like those wavering hopes of Aidenn,
Dimly in our dreams that lie;
Clouded often, drowned in turmoil,
Faint and lovely, far away —
Wreathing sunshine on the morrow,
Breathing fragrance round today.
Love would wander
Here and ponder.
Hither poetry would dream;
Life's old questions,
Sad suggestions,
Whence and whither? throng thy stream.

On the roaring waste of ocean
Shall thy scattered waves be tossed,
'Mid thy surge's rhythmic thunder
Shall thy silver tongues be lost.

O' thy glimmering rush of gladness
Mocks this turbid life of mine!
Racing to the wild Forever
Down the sloping paths of Time!
Onward ever,
Lovely River,
Softly calling to the sea;
Time that scars us,
Maims and mars us,
Leaves no track or trench on thee.

- 1868

1 - The Introductions

Love is our true destiny. We do not find the meaning of life by ourselves alone-we find it with another.
Thomas Merton

I am Sarah Keys, a reluctant narrator of a story about my family who came to the West on the Oregon Trail in 1846. As the volunteer family historian, I am the logical spokesperson for the following story. I am not one to usually put myself out front. Others consider me shy, and I always prefer working in the background. I have worked with the family forever on the farmstead, store, and restaurant. I never put much thought into not working for the family as I always just placed that expectation on myself. Besides, I have loved being part of a family that showed determination to come West under the most profound hardships of the time. It was apparent when someone entered the old store, now converted into a restaurant. The sounds of this old building that had been here since 1890 made a lot of noises, like the rattling of the doorknob and squeaky hinges, which let me know that we had a guest. Before this building was here, it was a family homestead, and for fifty years, the Keys family had tilled the soil in hopes of achieving the dream that the family patriarch had as he and his wife came here on the Oregon Trail.

He strode in with a cautious look and told the waitress that he was waiting for someone. He looked like he was in his forties with green eyes, dark hair, and stubble that would make any farmer proud. He sat there seemingly thinking deeply, but it also appeared to me that there was sadness in his face. It occurred to me that something about him seemed familiar, but that thought disappeared quickly. I overheard him talking to Jan, who was waiting tables, and he gave his name as Jessie Randall. He closed his eyes as if he was resting, shuddered, and upon opening his eyes, he was looking directly at me. He smiled, and I blushed while backing out of the room.

After about fifteen minutes, another man entered and walked over to Jessie. He was hesitant but introduced himself as Harrison Holmes. Jessie reached out to shake his hand and, with a smile, said welcome cousin. I have been looking forward to talking to you. As they went about their conversation, I returned to focusing on my work and would occasionally notice that Jessie was looking at me but chose to ignore him.

I could tell they were in a deep conversation, and I did overhear that they were getting to know each other for the first time, so I left them alone and went about my work.

Jessie thought catching up on each other's lives would be a good idea as they only recently found each other online.

Harrison agreed and asked Jessie to start. Jessie took a breath and started the conversation about his childhood. He said, I learned at a very early age that I was different from other kids in that I could sense and feel things that I didn't understand, which developed over the years into hearing and seeing things. Of course, as a kid, I thought everyone could do these things, and I would get into trouble by blurting out what I was aware of. I couldn't understand the looks that people would give me. My parents admonished me for speaking up. I will provide you with an example. We were a very Catholic family, and I remember sitting in church watching the congregation at four years old. I don't know why I said it, but I looked at my mother and said out loud that the man in the next pew would die. Everyone in earshot looked in my direction and then at my mother. She told me to be quiet and, after the service, told me never to repeat those things. I, of course, didn't understand what was wrong. It turns out the man did die, and it put my Catholic family on edge with everyone else in trying to deflect comments about a kid who could see and feel things. I remember learning quickly that the general population did not see these things and that I had to keep what I saw to myself if I didn't want to appear different. Understanding this at a very early age made me constantly aware that telling the truth wasn't a great idea because it resulted in punishment that seemed unfair.

I always saw energy as moving dots or bubbles. There were no solid walls because I could sense I could walk through them. Unfortunately, it took a couple of broken bones to realize that what I saw was different from what was physical to my body. Even as a kid, it takes little to make a good lesson.

While growing up, I wanted to be quite normal, so I learned to place these experiences into a box that, over time, I opened very seldom. It wasn't until I became an adult that I could no longer ignore the overwhelming amount of what I now know as Intuitive skills. So, it came to a point where I made a conscious decision to open the box for good and enter this unseen world with complete conscious understanding despite my Catholic upbringing. I realized I had suppressed a lot from childhood, including playing with the Angels. They told me a long time ago that there would be a time when these skills would be more accepted in this world, and I would use them for the good of all. I have always thought that restricting and controlling kids who show skills outside of the box was detrimental to them. Still, when you are young, you try so hard to fit into society, but it is no wonder that there are so many confused and damaged souls on this planet. That is a bit of my background. How about you, Harrison? What has been your storyline besides having sisters that were related generations back?

 Wow, that is quite a story. It is impressive that you could understand that early on and protect yourself from ridicule. I am impressed. My story is not so dramatic.

 Like you, as a kid, I knew that there was more going on in life than what was happening around me. I remember thinking about Heaven probably when I was five, and strangely thinking it would have been too crowded if people hadn't recycled. I thought, what a strange thing for me to think about. I could have been a better student because I focused less than my teachers wanted me to. That was obvious when I discovered report cards growing up, which showed I was more of a social butterfly than someone focused on grades. As I grew up, I was following the dots in life. I didn't necessarily plan my future but was happily going with the flow. My family was more like "Leave it to Beaver," and my parents expected me to graduate. So, it all seemed perfect. At one point, I went to junior college and became a journalist without experience, just because it seemed fitting. I went into the business world for the same reason. I studied things that interested me, like Yoga, and I was always interested in learning about esoteric fields mainly because I just knew there had to be more out there. Over my lifetime, I have had different experiences, like seeing and hearing things, but never continuously. These random events and my aptitude for following what was before me eventually led me to write. Why not, right?

Even though something does not make sense to those around you, I have always believed you should follow your heart. If it feels right and you are not hurting anyone but yourself, then making sense of things gives empowerment to achieve those things that come up in a life that only you see as important. It felt right when you contacted me, and we realized we were related. Your skill levels in your Spiritual growth and mine in writing are a perfect match. I am interested in understanding things that happened to me and feel that our relationship is a safe space to do that. I hope I can help you express things you have never been able to do in a way that makes you feel safe as well. Therefore, this is a perfect steppingstone for both of us, and I look forward to

1 – The Introductions

where this is going.

 I do not know how long I have worked here, but it seems like forever. I remember being around this area that the restaurant sat on for years, as the seasons changed yearly. I loved being here in the country and being around people who worked here and our many customers who came to think of this place as a second home. It is where the floorboards are worn into smooth patterns by all the years of people walking back and forth, to the sound of laughter and the smells of cooking. It is a beautiful place to watch a family grow up and spread out in all directions of the compass. I think it all started because the tales of the Oregon Territory sounded too good to be true, and my family joined thousands of other hardy souls looking for a better life in the West. I am proud to be from such stock.

 I was going to clean a table and was shocked as I turned around and Jessie was standing there. Startled, I inched back, but he raised his hand and apologized. He did not mean to scare me but wanted to know if he could ask me questions about the building and the history of this site. Looking into his eyes, I do not know why, but I sensed a feeling of safety, so I decided to follow him to the table and sit with them.

 Jessie introduced me to Harrison and told me that he was a writer of some growing fame and, through family research, found out that they were cousins and had mutual interests, including history, the Oregon Trail, and other issues. Jessie told me that since childhood, he was what some folks called gifted because he could sense things that others could not. Although it made his childhood awkward, these gifts slowly and carefully developed into a business where people could have positive outcomes. He told me he developed skills over his lifetime that allowed him to talk to Spirts and use his intuitive gifts of sight, sound, feeling, and knowing to accept that he was here to help people. He spoke to Harrison and said to him that he thought that they could join forces, he could use his skill set, and Harrison could write about the place and time.

That is all interesting, but I could not see what he needed me for until he turned to me and said, that is where you come in. He said that he knew that I had been around here a long time and probably knew the history of this place as well as anyone else. He said he has been dreaming of this site and feels like he is being drawn to it. He explained that when he has dreams three times, he pays attention to them. That usually means to him that he needs to do something about it. That is why he is here, and when his cousin contacted him about these mutual interests, he took it to mean more than just a coincidence.

1 – The Introductions

He asked me if it would be okay to drop in over the next few months and ask questions about the original homestead, the store and restaurant, and anything I could remember to fill in the story's color. He told me he would never abuse his time here or create a story that was not true. He wanted the story to be genuine, and as he looked over to Harrison, who shook his head in agreement, he said that he had wasted enough of my time and would return in a couple of days if that was okay. I thought about it, decided I felt comfortable enough to continue our conversation, and told him I looked forward to it.

Queen City of the Trails

Imagine after you have decided to venture to the West on one of the many trails to Oregon, California, Santa Fe, or other points to start a new life. Not only was the decision hard in the first place, but you had to figure out all the logistics to get there. Oh, and you had to account for the costs. But once you have reached that decision, you must decide where to start. In most cases in 1846, that involved getting to the little town of Independence, Missouri, by boat or other means of transportation. You had a wagon made when you reached Independence or came fully outfitted from wherever you started. But Independence was, for the most part, in the beginning, the jumping-off point for going West.

Of course, single men and women, as well as extended families, made these hard decisions. The conjunctive point centered around this little town of Independence was, at the time, the western edge of civilization for the young United States. It started with a few hundred people and got its name from the Declaration of Independence. Because it was the furthest point on the Missouri River where larger boats could safely come west, it was a natural point of departure. Independence grew into a hub of activity, attracting many businesses and those with the skills to help the growing numbers of those wishing to go West. These included wagon makers, merchants, blacksmiths, and any businesses that followed commerce of the opening of new lands.

There was a lot of money to be made off these travelers, especially during the early Spring as they all got ready to head out after the Winter thaw and the growth of plants to feed the animals pulling these wagons. If they left too soon, there wouldn't be enough feed, and they took the chance of getting bogged down in mud along the way. If they left too late, they risked not getting over the Rocky Mountains before the snow came in. Living in this time brought all kinds of risks for people, but the risks increased for an adventure like this.

And so, they came in numbers that grew yearly until train travel became possible in the late 1860s. What these immigrants saw and felt in Independence had to be eye-opening, especially if they came from big cities in the East.

They would have seen a very active frontier town with lots of noise from the many blacksmiths and other establishments, as well as the places that didn't necessarily lend themselves to some of the strong family convictions of these travelers. The amusement for the children would have been substantial and probably be of great concern for some adults.

This little frontier town was on the map for the Spaniards who came through early, the French fur traders, and the establishment of the Santa Fe Trail after the Louisiana Purchase in 1803.

Mormon missionaries came to the area in 1830 to hopefully convert the local Indians and established a base of operation until 1833, when the non-Mormons rose in dispute and, through various skirmishes, forced the Mormons to move out of the area. Before the Civil War, this area was building in its dismay over the tensions within the United States about slavery. So, there would have been no doubt that in 1846, the immigrants arriving and going through this part of the country would have felt a tension building no matter their personal beliefs. All of this made for stress and theatrics that helped grow this town.

Leaving Independence in fully loaded wagons can only be imagined as exciting on the one hand, but there would have been a cloud of apprehension as well. What were they getting into, and would they survive what had to be the naivete needed to have such an adventure?

2 - The Journey Begins

Much of the country within two hundred miles of the Ocean, is favorable to cultivation. The valley of the Multnomah is particularly so, being extremely fertile. The advantages, generally, for acquiring property are paramount to those on the prairies of the West or in any other part of the world. Oregon is covered with heavy timber forests. The production of vegetables, grain, and cattle will require comparatively but little labor; these articles, together with the spontaneous growth of the soil, and the fruits of laborious industry, in general, will find a market, at home, and thereby comfort and enrich the settlers. Surplus staple articles maybe shipped from their doors to distant ports and return a vast profit in trade. Lumber, ship timber, may be sent to the western coast of South America, the islands in the

Pacific; bread stuffs, furs, salmon, and many other articles of domestic manufactures, to the East Indies.
Hall J Kelley - 1839

Time went by as I worked around the restaurant, and although I didn't think about Jessie's request too much, it was in the back of my mind, and for some reason, I felt excited about the thought of seeing them both again. I do not spend much time considering my appearance, but I wanted to present myself well. I have fair skin and blond hair and always dress well, but I do not feel the need to put on air about my appearance. But, then again, it is nice to have someone showing attention, so I wanted to do my best. It has been a while since I have been interested in that area.

As promised, Jessie and Harrison arrived together and looked more comfortable than the last time I saw them. They took a seat and invited me over to talk. I finished what I was doing and decided that I could take a break from my duties while simultaneously enjoying the thought of participating in something different. I sat down and noticed that Harrison had a paper pad in front of him, and Jessie asked if it would be okay if he took notes to remember what I said. It will help with the story development. I told him I did not have a problem with it. So, we began our meetings over several visits

2 – The Journey Begins

during the next few months.

As fascinating as their company, it was even more enjoyable for me to share the stories of the Keys family in their migration on the Oregon Trail and the trials and tribulations of establishing a homestead over the years as the family got more significant in size and they developed not only a farm but the business opportunities that followed. I had become a family historian, so I mentally kept track of all the records of births and deaths and the backgrounds of those in the family. So, it was easy for me to share that with Jessie and Harrison, as I loved the whole challenging story of the incredible journey of those who came from the East in the great migration.

Jessie asked if we could start at the beginning, so he asked if any stories in the family talked about why they decided to go West in the first place.

I understood that in the 1830s, there was a financial panic back East, and my family had debt they couldn't cover. So, like many families, they chose to go West to escape the panic's devastating effects. Also, they said Hall J. Kelley put out information in 1831 that discussed the benefits of moving to the Oregon Territory. He made it so appealing to my family that they got excited about the possibilities. Of course, the writers of these early stories did not convey the hardships very well, so they went into it somewhat blinded by the possibility of providing a better future for the family. My ancestors came from Illinois and headed to Independence, Missouri, to be part of the 1846 caravan, which consisted of sixty-three wagons, one hundred nineteen men, fifty-nine women, one hundred ten children, and all the supplies and animals needed to take care of that many people. I know from stories that this group increased and decreased in size over the journey because groups would join in various places or leave to go in different directions.

There was even a story about the Donner party joining my family's group after they got to the encampment around the Kansas border. Of course, the Donner party went through terrible times after turning south towards California, and my family went to Oregon.

Harrison asked if I knew what the people in the family's group were like. I said that I gathered from conversations over the years that the wagon train consisted of all kinds: families, individuals, men, women, and children from all walks of life.

There were older adults that they thought would never make it, as well as some questionable characters that they had to keep an eye on. They passed down one story about a gentleman named Patrick Brennan, who had a lousy reputation involving drinking and getting into fights. He caused my relatives a lot of hardship along the way, and at one point, a jury of the men in the camp had to be selected to deliver a verdict about something Patrick did. I understood that each Wagon Train elected its people to keep order, and injustices were dealt with swiftly. I don't know the whole story, but I am sure he was punished accordingly.

From the stories, I know that many people became good friends while on the journey. I can only imagine that it would have been hard work and lonely at times, especially since most of those people left their families behind and might never see them again.

Our family became remarkably close to a few families with children who could play together while the parents could talk about farming in the new territory. It helped pass the time, especially since it was a long journey. One of the families my family traveled with settled close to our homestead in Oregon. They became close in the years following. The story goes that they brought along a dog named Alder, and that dog adopted our family as well. Then, when they settled nearby, Alder became the community dog, and everyone loved him. The story goes that somewhere along the trail, this family had asked our family to take the dog as our own. I had never heard why, but it did not matter, as Alder decided he belonged to the community more than anyone. Having friends and animals along made the journey a little like the homes they came from and brought comfort in some way. At least, that is what I would like to think.

Jessie asked if I had heard about any story that upset the family.

I told him my family talked about an accidental death in our family, but they did it in hushed, reverend ways that the story never came out, so I do not know anything other than something happened. So much time has gone by that the stories have faded because no one can pass them down.

Jessie stretched and told Harrison that maybe that was enough for one day. He leaned towards me and said that he appreciated everything I had been sharing and that they would return soon for another round of discussions. I said that would be great and that I look forward to it. They both stood up and walked out the door with its usual squeaking noises sounding out.

The Fog
By Mike Russell

*Fighting the urge to forgive
something that I don't even recognize,
envelopes my desire
to understand that there is always
more to a story than the beginning.*

*The fog keeps you chained to an area
that doesn't reveal the secrets
or what is just outside the boundaries
of its protection.*

*The option to enter and look beyond the fog
never occurred to me
until the door opened
that was showing
the story has many endings.*

*Staying safe within the confines of the fog
isn't always a reflection of your past,
but it can be a redemption in your future.*

3 - Traveling Back into Time

Another rainy night and cloudy cold and uncomfortable morning. Mrs. Lancaster's child a daughter 16 months old died 10 o'clock. The doctor called the disease symptomatick fever accompanied with worms. Continues to rain moderately. May 21. After burying the child, we started and drove 6 miles.
Medorem Crawford - 1842

The next time I saw Jessie walk in, he was alone. He sat in his usual place and asked me if we could talk. I came over and sat down, and Jessie told me that Harrison was tied up with another project and could not make it. He asked me if recording this visit was okay so he could give the information to Harrison. I did not mind, so we began. He said that the last time we spoke, we talked about the people my ancestors met on the journey. Now, he wanted to know if there were stories about the journey.

I was told that the days were long and hard, from sunup to sundown in most cases. Women worked the camp area by cleaning, cooking, gathering wood, and such, while the men cared for the animals and hunted along the way. Not everyone could do everything, so there was a lot of sharing.

Over the years I have been here, I have found some of my ancestors' diaries, which have given me some details. For instance, one diary said it cost them about 800.00 to buy everything they needed to supply the wagon. That included the oxen for pulling the wagon and food staples to last the trip because, in this case, my family came out very early in the migration, and there were very few places to restock along the way. After I read that, I wondered who in the 1840s could have afforded to go West because of the cost of outfitting a wagon properly. Poor people back East might not be able to do it.

But I suppose if there was a strong will, there was possibly a way. Maybe relatives could lend them the funds in hopes of making money in the West or setting up a homestead that would eventually greet more relatives later. Walking was the most day-to-day exhausting part. On good days, they might cover fifteen miles, but on average, it was a lot less than that due to weather, terrain, sickness, and many other things that seemed to occur daily. They had many rivers to cross.

3 – Traveling Back into Time

Some were easy, where the animals could pull the wagons across, and some were treacherous, where the wagons had to be floated across while the animals swam. There were many instances when people drowned or died by the wagons falling on them. Most of all, some illnesses beset many, of which some did not survive.

I read in one of my ancestor's diaries that it seemed like there was a grave every mile. I am sure some of that was exaggerated, but much was true. Can you imagine seeing that and still needing to move on so you could make it before Winter sets in? They had to be such strong stock to ignore those types of sites. I am sure it caused quite a few mental breakdowns among the weaker. I sometimes wonder what people thought after they got so far away from where they left and realized that it was much more challenging. They probably felt trapped between turning around, returning, and sticking it out to make it to the West. Every day, so much fatigue and pain must have caused unimaginable anxiety and stress for everyone involved.

I overheard someone talking who said an estimated 400,000 came on the Oregon Trail, and about 80,000 settled in Oregon. The rest went North and South once they got here. That is many dreams and hopes riding on making it to a promised land you cannot rely on. I shudder sometimes at the thought of it. That is the story I know from what I have read and heard.

Jessie said you mentioned something that happened to someone in your family on the way, but the family did not want to discuss it. Have you ever been able to find out more of the story by reading the diaries?

I was always curious about that myself. I saw references to it in the diaries but never any detail. I have sometimes imagined being out there with everyone and trying to understand what happened. Jessie asked if we could try an experiment and imagine that I was there when it happened. See if I could reach out and touch the memories of my family. It seemed kind of silly to me, but since it was my family, we were talking about, it probably would not hurt. So, Jessie told me to close my eyes, and he slowly started talking to me through a scene of being on the Wagon Train on the day that something happened to my family. He asked me what I was seeing in my mind. Slowly, a picture of a bustling camp life came into my mind. I watched a woman standing in her wagon with a crying child in her arms. For some reason, the child could not be comforted. It looked feverish, and nothing was working to calm it. The woman also talked to Patrick Brennan, standing outside the wagon and complaining about the crying child. As usual, he had been drinking and wasn't a good person to be around in those circumstances. Patrick grabbed the baby and yanked her out of the woman's hands. The woman was yelling at him and for help. As Patrick backed up with the baby and the crowd of camp people were reacting to the screams, he tripped over the tongue of the wagon, "the pole that extends from a wagon between the animals that are attached to pull it," which was lying on the ground after the oxen had been unhitched and dropped the baby. The child hit its head on a rock by the front left wheel and stopped crying. Patrick stumbled backward away from the wagon and, realizing what had happened, ran from the oncoming crowd. The mother screamed as the baby's father ran over to pick the baby up. It was apparent to all that the baby was dead as all the women gathered around the mother to comfort her. Someone yelled to fetch the Doctor, and one of the older boys ran to look for him.

Several of the men chased after Patrick and caught him trying to mount a mule to get away. They tied him to the wheel of a wagon and went to the Wagon Master in charge of the train to discuss the circumstances. In the meantime, the Doctor had arrived, confirmed the death, and gave the mother a sedative to calm her nerves. The Wagon Train did not travel that day as preparations for a funeral were a priority. Also, a trial was convened between the men to decide the fate of

Patrick Brennan. The women of the Wagon Train created a funeral service for the baby while a man made a little box of hewn wood from a nearby tree. Towards three in the afternoon, somebody noticed that the mother was nowhere to be found. Everyone in the group started looking for her, and yelling came from the river. They all went down to the river to see a couple of men pulling the woman's body from the river. She had been so grief-stricken that she just walked into the river and drowned. So, that day in camp was sad for everyone as two funerals needed planning.

At the end of the day, as sunset was occurring, the minister of the Wagon Train said words over two graves of this mother and child. A stone marker was made with their names, ages, and dates at each foot.

Jessie broke in quietly and asked if I could see the names on the marker. I looked closely, and it read Sarah Keys and Adelaide Keys, ages thirty and one. They died on May 29, 1846. May they rest in peace. What?

I opened my eyes, startled by what I had just seen. It can't be.

That is my name. I am Sarah Keys. That must be where I got my name, but the scene was honest and emotional. I was so confused that I jumped up and backed away from the table. Jessie said he would return in a few weeks to discuss it more.

3 – Traveling Back into Time

I could not even answer him as he left the restaurant. I saw the scene spin around in my head and saw flashes of light and shifting pictures so much that I decided to lie down. I do not remember waking up for a long time.

The pain of the Keys family, especially the father, was something that I could not get out of my mind. I remembered details from my last visit with Jessie that made me feel lost. The look in the father's eyes after discovering his wife was dead, let alone his baby, was something I could not erase from my memory of that dream session with Jessie. I had no idea how much time had passed since our last meeting. The feelings of being there were so real I could smell the dirt and dust of the Wagon train. The sweat and tension in the air clung to me as if I had traveled back in time and could feel everything around that campsite. I cannot understand how trying to imagine an event could be so real that you could swear you were there. Pictures kept coming, like the funeral and subsequent trial of Patrick Brennan. It must have been something Jessie did to plant those thoughts in my mind, but I could not help but think there was more to it. All these scenes floating through were one thing, but the connection to my name was understood even less. My family here would have shared the origins of my name and let me know that my name came from someone on the Wagon Train. But it hurts to think that something like this would never be mentioned. Maybe they did not know because I could not understand why it would be a secret.

4 - The Reality

It is true that no general organization for law and order was effected on the western side of the river. But the American instinct for fair play and a hearing for everybody prevailed so that while there was not mob law, the law of self-preservation asserted itself, and the counsels of the level-headed older men prevailed. When an occasion called for action, a high court was convened, and woe betide the man that would undertake to defy its mandates after its deliberations were made public.

Ezra Meeker - recalling 1852

In this seemingly endless fog of thought, I noticed Jessie and Harrison entering the restaurant. I didn't know whether to acknowledge them or continue working. Still, my curiosity got the better of me, and I walked over to them and unloaded my confusion in a not-so-ladylike way, not allowing them to respond until I got my concerns off my chest. Jessie was quick to respond once I let him have a word edgewise. He said that our last meeting, although producing results that he was not expecting, was also profound for him. His dreams are highly charged, and he wanted to apologize for apparently opening a door that created so much stress for me. I told him that although I had been walking around in a daze with all these scenes in my head, I had concluded that I was curious enough to continue our conversation because it involved my family. I want to tie the stories I have heard all my life into a package that makes sense, especially how my name is linked to the woman in the wagon. I asked him if we could take it a little slower and gentler from now on. He agreed and filled in Harrison on what transpired last time as he could not be there. After Jessie set the scene as he remembered, Harrison said he understood how that could have shocked me and again pulled out the recorder for today's session.

Jessie thought it might be helpful to expand on the last session without the drama. He suggested I return but added that he would like to provide a safer way. I said okay. Again, through his gentle suggestions, he asked me to go back, but this time, he added that all will be viewed within the safety of someone just watching and not judging as if they are watching a movie. This gentle method of detachment allowed

4 – The Reality

me to return to that day and communicate with Jessie as it happened. He first asked what was going on. I said the Wagon Trail was preparing to move on, and all except the Keys were preparing for the continued trek. He asked me what was going on with the Keys. I told him that the Wagon Master was talking to the husband and father who lost his wife and child by calling him Peter. He said to take an extra day to be with his thoughts and grieve. Peter could easily catch up with the Wagon Train within a few days. Peter said that he appreciated it and would stay with his extended family for one extra day and meet the rest down the trail soon. I could tell that his grief was intense by the way Peter was standing and leaning over. He didn't have enough energy to start back on the trail immediately.

Jessie asked me if any other family members were around, and I noticed a few women and a couple of men with their children over by the wagon talking. I listened and realized they were talking about the deceased wife. One woman, whom I assumed was Peter's Aunt, said that Maybelle was fragile and felt that this trip would be too much for her no matter what happened. I got confused at this point because I thought her name was Sarah. She said her grandmother, whom they left in Illinois, asked us to watch out for Maybelle Sarah. I caught my breath and realized that the woman the incident was about went by Maybelle to her family, but she was known as Sarah to everyone else. So, that explains where my name came from. They quietly talked about Maybelle Sarah so Peter would not get upset more than necessary. The group's men suggested that from this point on, the family should say that her death was an accident and not speak of the real story behind her and the baby's death, as it wouldn't benefit anyone.

I thought that sounded stupid because the memories of these two lost souls would be forever assembled into a story of falsehoods. Of course, the men told the women that it would be the best for the family, and what looked like to me was subjugated to the men's wishes. Jessie asked me how I felt, and I said sad, but at the same time, I understood it. The conversation continued, and strangely, it turned into a discussion with the sister of Maybelle Sarah, Grace. She appeared to be a couple of years younger than Maybelle Sarah, and the conversation was about her taking up the role of her sister both for the family and Peter's sake. I was puzzled, except in the back of my mind, I have heard many stories of men taking up with deceased relatives after a loss. This way of thinking was common during those times, and Grace was a pretty thing who did not seem to be too upset with the idea. She even said they all grew up together and

4 – The Reality

would happily help Peter get to the West Coast. But Grace was not promising anyone that there would be more to it than that. After all, she was also grieving for her sister and niece, and they could comfort each other for the rest of the journey. Time will tell. They all agreed that it was best for everyone and would convey the correct story about an arduous but positive journey West instead of a tragic family event to the next generations. At least, that was what they were saying now. I could not accept that the future would delete references to these two souls.

Jessie asked if I could see what happened with the trial of Patrick Brennan. I looked around and did not see him around the campsite, but as I looked further out, I noticed a lone tree on a hill some distance away. To my horror, I could tell a body was hanging from the tree. I did not need to know anymore as I knew what happened, and according to Wagon Train, Justice, which I have heard about in the past, these kinds of things are dealt with quickly and harshly. Harrison spoke up, and I could hear him like he was far away. It was like someone in another room, and you could listen to them in a muffled way. He was saying that Wagon Train justice took many forms depending on the severity of the crime. Some people were banished from the train, some were turned over to the Forts they encountered, and some were punished immediately. He said that without the usual access to any court system, they had to deal with issues as they came up.

Causing a death was one of those crimes that resulted in the harshest punishment. It was horrible, but it was a sign of the times, and the Wagon Train agreed to the rules governing everyone's behavior at the beginning of each journey. None of the travelers would have been surprised that the court would have quickly handed out punishment.

Jessie asked me to come back slowly and safely without any concern about what I saw. I opened my eyes, looking straight into Jessie's eyes. He had concern etched on his face and asked me if I was okay.

I said yes and meant it because now I knew my family's story and where my name came from. I told him it helped fill in all the blanks and appreciated his concern. He looked at Harrison, and they both shook their heads, and I knew it was time for them to leave. It would give me a lot to think about until I saw them next time.

Immigrant Wagons

 Immigrants made many decisions, with the choice of wagons and what animals to pull one of the most critical. During the early years of traveling West, most wagons used were retrofitted farm wagons. However, as time passed, companies specializing in wagon building developed to sell to the increasing population moving West.

 Although the bigger Conestoga wagon was used in many Westerns, the smaller version was the workhorse of the Oregon Trail. Sometimes, it was called the prairie schooner because of the white canvas top. From a distance, it seemed like a boat on the ocean.

Other names for this wagon were white top or ambulance. It consisted of a box that had to carry everything that the immigrant needed.

The box typically measured 8 to 10 feet long, 4 feet wide, and 2 feet high on the sides. With the canvas top put on over the bows, the height was around 10 feet.

The pioneers had to be good at packing everything into that small space. Even if they were good at it, they often found that they had to scrap heavier objects on the trail, like stoves, chairs, and furniture, along the way because the heavy wagon would get bogged down in sand, rivers, and mud. They had to decide whether these items were worth the risk to their wagons and, most importantly, their lives. It could make the difference of making it to the West or not. So, even though grandma's heirlooms were important in the East, many items were left along the trail due to the risk factors involved.

As there was very little room in the wagon for people, most walked the 2000 miles and left the wagon riding to the sick and elderly.

Besides, it was so uncomfortable to ride in the wagon because there were no springs, so whoever tried to ride was bounced around so much that most people chose to walk. Also, during dust storms, it was almost impossible to be in an enclosed space that would cover anyone with layers of dust. Sleeping for most on the trail was outdoors, either in a tent, under the wagon, or just on the ground. If those traveling had the funds, having more than one wagon for a group would be possible, which would spread things out and give some space to those riding in the wagon. These folks were from hearty stock, so walking most of the trail was more pleasant than being stuck in the wagon.

Because the oxen were cheaper and had benefits like being more patient and obedient, they were selected to pull the wagons roughly eighty percent of the time over mules and horses. They also were more adaptable to prairie grasses and weren't particular in what they ate and drank. They were slower than horses or mules, but they held up better to the journey with their slow but steady pace. After all, the goal was to get to the West and not have to replace animals along the way. Most wagons had 4 to 6 oxen hooked up in pairs.

As with any trip planned in the 1840s or now, it takes planning of what to take and, most importantly, money. The costs could run from $500 to $1,000 per wagon for the supplies needed. For instance, they not only required wagons and draft animals but riding horses, cows for milk and cheese, saddles, blankets, tents, nails, soap, stoves, coffee, frying pan, knives, candles, wash tubs, tar buckets for axle grease, hand tools, rope, and weapons. They also took flour, salt, bacon, sugar, coffee, dried fruit, lard, vinegar, medicines, rice, beans, potatoes, and sometimes chickens and *turkeys. When they started, they either read the recommendations from books about how much to carry per person or received advice from those who had gone before.*

Remembering that this trip took 4 to 6 months to travel and that there were few places to buy supplies along the way, they needed to plan accordingly. Even if they made it to the various Forts on the trails, the costs tended to be high at the Fort stores. So, planning upfront was always better. If they traveled with large extended families, the costs rose exponentially, but they could share them.

5 – Truly into The West

After we left Missouri, all the buildings I remember seeing were Forts Laramie, Bridges and Hall. As this was but the second year of "Crossing the Plains," the way before us was much of it through a wilderness and over a trackless plain. There were no bridges, no ferries, and a stream too large to be forded was crossed by means of rafts, if there could be found timber along its banks to make rafts. If not, our wagon beds were used for flat boats."

Mary Elizabeth Munkers Estes - recalling 1846

The following weeks between our visits were the same mundane tasks around the restaurant that I always did. It is funny in a way because I never thought of what I did around here as ordinary until Jessie came into my life and introduced a story about the family. Ever since the last meeting, I have felt a need to go over and over the scenes I saw and the feelings that seemed a part of me now. I was having dreams when I was resting that was so profoundly real that sometimes I did not know if I was dreaming or not. My vision was also changing because I saw flashes of light sporadically, whether my eyes were closed or open. They appear to have a scene attached to them, and even though they flash for a split second, it always gives me a feeling of comfort. I find that odd since, in the past, it would scare me if I saw things like this. Most images embedded in these flashes involve the blurred image of someone lost and searching for something. Since it's not necessarily scary, I brought it up the next time I saw Jessie and Harrison.

I continually think about the hardships of my family on the Oregon Trail and all the families that traveled West in hopes of a better tomorrow. The naïve nature of doing something big had to be overwhelming to most of those folks. It would be unthinkable to entertain the idea of such a bold adventure, especially with an extended family. Marching through the elements daily for around five months to get to a place where you had no assurance that it would be better than where you came from seems crazy.

But, at the same time, I am also a little jealous as I fantasize about doing something bold and challenging in my life that could be a story passed down so many years later. I wonder what Maybelle Sarah would have been like if she had made it to the West Coast. Suddenly, a flash of light hit me, and I quickly sat down as it was making me dizzy. This time, a picture of a young Sarah showed her smiling and happy and talking to someone about leaving. She did not appear to be apprehensive at all. The feeling I got right then was of love for her husband and that she was willing to follow him no matter where it took her. As brief as the vision was, I received an overwhelming feeling of calmness and the realization that Sarah did what she wanted to do in following her path. I sat for a while, enveloped in Sarah's love for her husband, until the door opened, and two familiar people strode in.

Jessie looked at me quizzically and asked me what happened. I sidestepped his question and asked him what he was talking about. Jessie said that he knew something had happened because of the energy level around me. I forgot that he seems to have perceptive powers, and obviously, I can't hide things from him. He said he noticed a glow of peace and calm radiating from me and just knew. So, I filled him and Harrison in on what has been happening since our last meeting, especially my vision of Sarah just now. Harrison said, oh my God, what a beautiful thing to happen to you. He asked if I felt connected somehow to Sarah because of this.

I feel so much more alive because of these connections.

It is like a thread attached to the past; these emotions and feelings travel on. I can sense what happened in 1846 and relate to it now. I am supposed to know my family's whole story and communicate that to the two of you. It is an honor that I am allowed to participate, and I find it hard to focus on what I do here because I am so connected to the past.

It is both strange and exciting at the same time. Jessie mentioned that his dreams are getting stronger and stronger, and what I am finding out through my experiences is helping to fill in the story he is getting. We are on a joint quest of some kind. He asked if I felt strong enough to continue with a new line of questioning or needed more time. I said I wanted to continue because it was essential to see where this goes.

With that, Jessie asked me to focus on a time when there was enjoyment along the trail. He reminded me there would be no stress, and I would view the scenes with detachment. One of my light flashes happened, and I was standing next to the Wagon Train as it was moving over a wide-open prairie. I could hear Jessie's voice as if from a distance, asking me to look around and describe what I saw. I realized that I was standing next to the Keys wagon, and I told Jessie that there was a cloud of dust rolling up from the other wagons, but I saw what looked like a building in the distance with a whole lot of color around it, but I couldn't make it out yet. I told him

5 – Truly into The West

I would walk along with the others, and when we get closer, I will describe what it is. So, that is what I did. Talk about being in the middle of the action. I often imagined what it would be like to be part of a Wagon Train, but this was amazing. I saw a lot of weary people and animals who were covered in dust following a well-worn trail. I heard someone yell that the Fort was up ahead, and suddenly, life began to flow into everyone.

It was as if they were all waking up from a dream and realizing where they were. I could see now that there was a Fort up ahead, and I overheard someone say that it was Fort John by the Laramie River, but I also heard that most folks call it Fort Laramie. It was on a vast open plain not close to the river. As we got closer, I realized that the color was not coming from the Fort but from a city of teepees and Indians camped around the Fort. I guess that there are hundreds of teepees. As I conveyed this scene to Jessie, I told him it was beautiful. There are a couple of thousand Indians, all decorated in colorful paint and dress.

The males are magnificent, but the women are so beautiful with their handmade clothing and feathers, and most have their hair pulled back. I feel something so profound that it is hard to tell Jessie, but I let him know that I feel flutters in my body as if I am being charged by what I see. It is taking my breath away. As we pull up to the Fort, I pull away from the scene out front and describe what the Fort looks like. It is impressive, with two of what I call guard towers at opposite corners. The height of the adobe walls is around fifteen feet high. The front of the Fort currently has two gates open. Above the gates is a large square room with two holes for what I would guess would be defensive. The gates open into an entryway that is closed by another inner gate with an opening high up where a person is talking to someone below. He yells to open the inner gate and let the Wagon Train folks in. Again, these all are ways to protect the Fort.

The inner gate opens, and I see it is divided in half, with the offices, sleeping quarters, officials on the left, and the blacksmith, horses, and cattle on the right. The size of the Fort is small compared to modern standards, but it is likely imposing on the emigrants who travel the Oregon Trail as it is the closest they have come to civilization in the last four hundred miles. One of the things I noticed walking in was that small cannons were sticking out of the holes above the entrance. Even though they are not huge, they would do an excellent job defending the Fort if needed. Jessie asked what else I could describe. Things were getting busy inside the Fort with the Wagon Trains' arrival. Wagon wheels were being repaired. Animal care was another thing I noticed, and the store, if it could be called that, was overrun by the women of the Wagon Train, mostly looking to replace supplies.

I hear some complaining about the prices, but considering this is in the middle of nowhere, they can probably charge and receive whatever they want. There is a little commotion going over by the store, so I decide to go over and see what is happening. There is a woman who is pregnant and surrounded by other women. They are talking to James Bordeaux, Fort Laramie's person in charge. They are saying that this woman, whose name is Charlotte, through no fault of her own, was attacked and became pregnant while traveling. The man was convicted by his peers and thrown out of that Wagon Train. Earlier in the trip, Charlotte's husband had died, leaving her alone with no one to help her get to Oregon. Being pregnant has created a hardship for her and everyone on the Wagon Train. One of the women asked James Bordeaux if he would allow Charlotte to stay at the Fort while she gave birth. After the birth, she could decide whether to continue going West the next season or find someone to help guide her back to the East. Mr. Bordeaux could see that Charlotte was distressed and said he would accept her into the Fort. He said that he only had fifteen men working for him, and they would be coming and going as they traded with Indians and trappers all over, so Charlotte would have to, for the most part, take care of herself and the baby. She will also need to work off the cost of room and board until she decides where and when she can move on. Mr. Bordeaux looked directly at Charlotte to ensure she knew what she was getting into. Charlotte nodded in agreement, and with that, Mr. Bordeaux introduced Charlotte to his wife, Marie, who he explained was his second wife. She was the sister of the Brule Lakota Chief Swift Bear. Her Indian name is Huntakalutawin. Charlotte looked into Marie's gentle eyes and smiled, not quite as afraid as she had been before. Marie smiled back at Charlotte and held out her hand. Charlotte took Marie's hand and led her away to help her settle in. The women of the Wagon Train thanked James Bordeaux for his kindness and departed to do what they needed to do at camp.

Jessie asked if I was okay, and I said I had witnessed a great act of kindness in a place where you would think it would be hard to come by. I looked around the inside of the Fort and described that the living quarters were built next to the Fort walls. I could tell that they were made high enough that they allowed people to use the roofs to walk along the length of the inside wall, giving the occupants a way to see what was going on outside the Fort with protection behind the adobe walls.

I heard that the date was June 27th, 1846, and the plan

5 – Truly into The West

was for the Wagon Train to be repaired and restocked until after the July 4th celebration. They planned to leave on the 6th and head towards the trail's midway point, the Rocky Mountains. I walked over to the Keys group, and they were talking about how excited they were to be able to celebrate the country on the 4th. They talked about how they had been hiding bottles of liquor in the wagons just for this occasion. I saw Peter Keys talking to two men by the store and decided to find out what was happening. One of the men introduced himself as Jed Compton. Jed said he needed a ride to Oregon and would work for his keep.

He said that his wagon had broken down, and he had to sell all his supplies to stay at this Fort until he could arrange another way to get to Oregon. He said he was a hard worker and that Peter would not regret it. Peter seemed to balk at the request but said he would consider it and let Jed know. They parted company, and Peter went over to the blacksmith shop to find out if the blacksmith had time to work on one of his wagon wheels that seemed to be loose. I decided I had seen enough for now, and I could hear Jessie and Harrison say it was time to call it a day. I returned to the restaurant with so many memories of the scenes that I just left and wanted to spend some time thinking about everything. I said goodbye to Jessie and Harrison and told them I would see them next time.

What Could Happen?

What could happen?

It is only a two-thousand-mile trip across the country, including deserts, mountains, rivers, and all bone-rattling surfaces. What could go wrong?

Luckily, if a pioneer took any advice before leaving and paid attention to this advice, they would have carried tools to repair just about anything that could happen. The wagon was so important to them that they needed to take all their supplies and use them in emergencies for the elderly, sick, and, of course, their kids. We all know that when you bring kids on a trip, there are bound to be many issues that pop up. So, off they went with their newfound information, praying that nothing would ever happen. Well, guess what, things happen.

5 – Truly into The West

The wagon wheels took an incredible amount of abuse and required constant attention. They not only had to check to ensure the wheels were not going to fall off, but they also had to ensure that they maintained the proper amount of grease to keep it rolling. This meant that every one to two days or thirty or forty miles, they had to jack the wheels up, clean off the old grease, and reapply new grease. It is like repacking the wheel bearings on a car now; it only has to be done a lot. They all carried a covered grease bucket with tar and grease that usually hung off the back of the wagon by the back wheels.

But that wasn't the only thing they had to worry about concerning the wheels. Because the spokes of the wheel were wood, and depending on who made the wagon and whether the wood was aged hardwood, there was a probability that the wood would dry out and crack. It posed a problem in that if this happened, especially if they were a long way from a Fort, for instance, then the wheels could collapse. Another duty was to inspect the wheels daily to ensure they weren't loose and even soak them in water to keep them from drying out. A metal ring was installed around the outside of the wheel to add stability and take the bulk of the bouncing around on the Oregon Trail. If anything happened to the metal ring, a wheelwright could fix it if they were at a Fort. But, of course, Forts were few and far between, so they had to get creative with wedges to keep things tight.

Creativity was needed to address all the issues that could happen to a wagon, and they sometimes had to resort to inventing answers as they went because there were mishaps that even advice books couldn't predict. Like today, with cars, frequent inspections and catching problems before they become significant issues are vital as they allow the person to keep the issues under control. But we all know that not everyone is cut from the same cloth, and some folks will always be more detailed than others. I imagine those more detail-oriented would have a better chance of getting to the West with fewer breakdowns than those who tend to ignore issues until they become major events. People are people in all periods, so at least carrying the standard tool kits, usually placed on the front of the wagon, could help in times of need. And maybe there were traveling companions that would have been handier with tools to help them when needed. That was always one of the reasons for traveling in larger groups. They could share the chores and repairs to get the whole group to the West. The learning curves of all these pioneers, whether men, women, or children, had to be rather steep, and if they didn't already know things from being farmers or other professions before they left, they learned quickly to survive along the Oregon Trail. There is something about learning on the job. After all, the consequences of not learning created high stress and a risk that would have overwhelmed anyone traveling. Life or death depended on focusing on the details.

6 – The National Celebration

West of Fort Laramie two emigrant parties, one of Edwin Bryant and the other of Lillburn Boggs, ex-governor of Missouri, held a conventional Independence Day celebration in a grove. A salute, a procession, the reading of the Declaration, a collation "served up by the ladies," toasts with a discharge of musketry after each, and patriotic songs constituted the program. J. H. Reed, of the Bryant party, had preserved wines and liquors, especially for the occasion.

Edwin Bryant, 1849 - reflecting on July 4, 1846

I spent the next few weeks doing what I always do around the restaurant, but in my spare time, I reviewed what I had seen at Fort Laramie. This bastion of commerce out in the middle of nowhere was one of the few places the pioneers had to look forward to other than the sometimes-beautiful country they were going through. It was almost like an oasis in the middle of a desert—a place for rest, recovery, and fixing things that would allow them to move on. The men seemed not to care too much but focused on getting everything done. The women seemed excited, on one hand, to be somewhere that reminded them of civilization, but I could see on their faces the concern that what lies ahead might be a lot more than what they bargained for. Even though they all had that naïve approach to this journey, they had to know that the journey was not even halfway, and there were mountains ahead that would make what they had already passed through seem tame in comparison. The children did not seem to show any interest in what the parents were doing unless they were doing chores. They only wanted to explore the Fort inside and outside and watch the Indians. Some of the Indian children were also curious, and, like everywhere, children played games with each other until the parents pulled them away for one reason or another. Some families were so worried about the Indian presence that they would keep their families close by and protected.

In contrast, the Keys family seemed more open to differences and allowed the intermingling among the Indians. There was little difference between what I see now around the restaurant area and then. Families are families; they all have

6 – The National Celebration

risk tolerances and concerns about so-called different people. It is interesting how things never change even after one hundred and seventy-plus years.

Time passed, and Jessie and Harrison walked in again with a smile and told me they were happy to see me. I told them the same. Jessie said that the last time I was at the Fort, I described the outside and inside and even listened in on a couple of conversations. He asked if it would be okay to go back there to see what was going on for the celebration of the 4th of July. It might be interesting to witness that kind of celebration. I agreed, and with that and the usual light flash, I found myself back at the Fort. No one was working that day as they all seemed excited and gathered at the Wagon Train. The group appeared much larger, and I saw another Wagon Train set up not too far away. It looked like this celebration involved everyone from both groups. I could see makeshift tables set up with food and drink and whatever decorations were found on the prairie. People from the Fort who work there were also coming out of the Fort to join in the festivities, as well as many of the Indians and their children, whom many in the Wagon Trains had gotten to know since I was last here. Everyone participating dressed in the best clothes they had. I noticed that gifts were given between the Indians, the people in the Fort, and the Wagon Train folks. The day was to be a celebration for all people. Even though I am sure that the 4th of July wasn't a day that Indians understood or would necessarily agree with, it did seem like everyone was relaxed enough that they all could have a good time.

I saw some of the men hiding the liquor bottles, which made me want to yell at them, but the times being what they were, it seemed like it was a normal reaction. I told Jessie and Harrison that it looked like the party was getting into full swing as some of the men were making speeches. When they finished, suddenly, musical instruments, including a violin and a drum made from various kinds of animal hide, came out, and dancing started in earnest. It is lovely to see that even for a short time, these pioneers who not too long ago were stressed beyond imagination were now showing a fun side and enjoying themselves as everyone was at least trying to dance, and that included the children and Indians close by. This one day, the world could slow down, and these people could forget about all the trials and tribulations in their everyday lives. The sights and sounds were so much fun to see that I turned circles in rhythm to the music. I heard Harrison saying that most of the Wagon Trains tried to time their arrival here so they could celebrate for a few days. The stop at the Fort not only allowed them time to restock and repair but also observing the birth of the country here at the

6 – The National Celebration

Fort seemed appropriate to these weary travelers as it wasn't lost on anyone that if it wasn't for that war against the British, this expansion Westward would look different.

Jessie asked what else I was seeing. I looked around and noticed that Peter Keys was walking away from the festivities and was walking with Jed Compton. That was odd since everyone had such a good time, so I followed them. I overheard Jed talking loudly to Peter and telling him that he had heard that he was escaping debts owed in the East, which is why his family was on the Wagon Train. At that moment, he demanded that he be allowed to go along with the Keys family, or he would get this information to the authorities. They knew the Army had dragged people off the Wagon Trains going West when they found out, so they could not escape their responsibilities.

Peter did not know how Jed had found out but looked scared enough that he said Jed could come along under one condition. He was not to mention this to anyone, including his family, as he did not want to upset them. And if he found out that Jed shared this information, there would be consequences.

Jed did not look threatened but said he would agree and join them on the trail on the seventh when they left. They both parted company, but I could see in Peter's eyes that he was concerned and shaken. He also seemed like he had no choice in the matter.

I returned to the celebration and told Jessie and Harrison they were serving food now that the speeches and dancing were completed. I stayed around, watched the groups enjoy the little food, and saw some men sneaking drinks by the wagons. It was interesting to watch the interplay between the various groups: Indians, children, and one dog named Alder, who seemed to be adopted by everyone.

What a joyous event. My thoughts returned to the conversation I overheard, and I hoped that Jed Compton would not cause trouble for the Keys family during the rest of the journey. As I was thinking that, I heard gunshots, which startled me until I realized that many men were shooting into the air to finalize the celebration of the 4th of July. By that time, the Indians had retreated to their camps, so it was just the last throws of a day that would probably have to last the rest of the journey, as I doubted that there would be another celebration until they made it to the West. With that, I returned to Jessie and Harrison, and we talked briefly about what I had seen and the feelings and emotions of those involved. I told them I was tired, and we agreed to meet in two weeks. We said our goodbyes, and I watched them leave the restaurant.

If It Won't Kill You, It Will Make You Stronger

One thing is sure: risk levels on the Oregon Trail were high. If the travel, wagons, animals, guns, weather, and people did not make you sick or kill you, then the extensive assortment of diseases and illnesses could make it extremely hard for a pioneer to get to the West.

Out of the 350,000 people who made the trip, diseases possibly claimed 30,000 lives, which equates to at least ten deaths per mile. The main culprits for diseases were Cholera, Scurvy, Dysentery,

Smallpox, Influenza, Measles, Mountain Fever, and other names. Because of the lack of knowledge in the 1800s, doctors were not always trusted, and pioneers tended to use granny remedies handed down through the families. It wasn't until the 1860s that the medical field started to tie germs to some diseases. Until then, they were basing their so-called cures on balancing the body through the theory of the Four Humors. Used to cure these diseases were bleeding, laxatives, and emetics to induce vomiting—mercury, arsenic, opium, vinegar, castor oil, and carbonate of magnesia. Plants and herbs like lobelia, juniper berries, and tree bark also played a role, along with peppers and garlic.

You did not want to go to a hospital for treatment in those days because of the likelihood that you would get sicker by being in the hospital. So, there were several self-help books during the time with home remedies. Take that thought process on a two-thousand-mile overland trail and multiply that by all the risks; it was more than likely that a considerable percentage at least got sick along the way and were lucky to get better. Some diary stories reflect on families being decimated by one illness or another. If you didn't have friends and family to help, there was a high likelihood that you could have been left to your own devices by the wagon train you were traveling with because they did not want to get sick as well. If left behind, you either got better or were never heard from again. Sometimes, parents died, leaving their children with other people *who might have been willing to take them in. Depending on the severity of the contagion, it would have been a torturous decision to take in someone who could have a disease that would affect the new family. Hard and impossible decisions like this were a daily trial.*

7 – The Depths of Grief

A black hole like a wound opened up in the sky last night, but I'm the only one who saw. In the dark, as I stood by myself, staring up at the stars and mourning Clara's death, still so fresh in my mind, it seemed as if God himself had torn a hole in the universe to pluck her soul like a flower…But look at me, writing all fancifully.

Elias J. Miller - 7/16/1846

Suddenly, with a jolt of energy, I found myself away from the wagon train, standing in a grassy prairie, facing a towering rock formation. I had arrived at this scene without going through the usual routine guided by Jessie. Overcoming my shock, I embraced the experience and saw where it would lead me. But why here? So, as in previous sessions, I absorbed my surroundings, committing them to memory so I could later recount them to Jessie and Harrison.

I strolled toward the rock formation, kicking up dust from the sandy soil while observing the prairie grass swaying in the wind. There was an inexplicable sense of importance about this place, yet all I could see were endless blue skies and red rocks. As I drew nearer, I noticed names and dates carved or painted onto the rock surface, created by the immigrants who had passed through here. These dates spanned a significant period, revealing a desire among these travelers to leave a mark, a testament to their existence, knowing they would likely never return.

Noise emanated from around a curve in the rock, and as I moved closer, I discovered Peter Keys sitting on the ground, hunched over as if in pain. My heart ached for him, realizing I had stumbled into his private grief. Initially, I contemplated leaving, but I decided to stay knowing he was unaware of my presence. Tears streamed down his face, a clear reflection of a broken man who hadn't had the opportunity to release the pent-up sadness since the loss of his wife and child, Adelaide. He uttered Sarah's name aloud, causing me to startle, thinking he was addressing me.

Of course, he was conversing with his departed wife. Peter expressed profound regret, blaming himself for their tragic fate. He apologized to Sarah, lamenting his inability to protect her and their baby. It was evident that Peter held

7 – The Depth of Grief

himself responsible for all that had unfolded. He was feeling angry, not only at himself but also with Sarah for leaving him. The weight of his grief and the overwhelming absence of his beloved threatened to consume him. My gut wrenched as if struck, dizziness and nausea washing over me. These intense sympathetic feelings and my solitary arrival in this place left me feeling somewhat out of control.

Collecting myself, I took a deep breath, gradually regaining composure.

Peter continued speaking to Sarah, expressing gratitude for her sister Grace's assistance in shepherding everyone to Oregon. Despite acknowledging Grace's kindness, he recognized she could never replace Sarah. Peter surmised that he and Grace would part ways once they reached their destination.

Suddenly, he erupted angrily, venting at Sarah's absence and his wavering faith. It appeared that grief had consumed him to question the strong faith that had initially motivated him and Sarah to embark on this journey. He deemed the current situation a deviation from their plan, feeling like he was drowning in a sea of misplaced thoughts.

Overwhelmed, Peter collapsed into a heap, his head buried between his legs. Tears fell onto the red dirt, forming a tiny pool before vanishing into the ground. He shuddered, raising his gaze and apologizing for his outburst. Believing he was more controlled than this, he expressed his desire to make Sarah proud. Taking a deep breath, he wiped away his tears. At that moment, a figure caught my peripheral vision. A silhouette approaching Peter. It was Grace.

She sat beside him, gently clasping his hand and whispering words of reassurance. She had overheard his conversation with Sarah and recognized a vulnerability she hadn't witnessed before. Grace revealed her grief, feeling as if she were merely going through the motions of daily life, lost in a fog of numbness. Until now, she had believed she was grieving alone.

Realizing that the burden of losing a loved one should not be faced in isolation, she extended her love and empathy toward Peter.

Grace professed her love for her sister and shared her grief for Sarah and Adelaide. She felt a profound connection with this man, sensing a moment of deep understanding and acceptance between them. Peter acknowledged the significance of remembering Sarah and Adelaide. They decided to honor their memories, not just dwelling on the tragedy but also sharing stories about them to keep their memory alive. Peter understood that the rest of their family thought it best not to discuss it openly out of a protective instinct. However,

7 – The Depth of Grief

he recognized his need to talk about it to prevent himself from descending into madness. They agreed that between the two of them, they would cherish and preserve those memories while also appeasing the rest of the family. Peter gazed at Grace, proposing they leave a lasting memory on this rock, visible to the world so other travelers would remember them in the future. Grace embraced the idea with love, and Peter picked up a rock from the red sand at their feet, etching an inscription into the face of the hard surface they sat upon. This rock, he explained, was Independence Rock, marking the halfway point to Oregon. With determination, Peter scratched and chipped the words, "For Sarah and Adelaide, you made it halfway, and we will carry you in our hearts the rest of the way. Grace Ames and Peter Keys - 1846." As the sun descended, casting an orange glow upon the inscription, they rose from their spot and headed back to the wagon train for the night. With a newfound commitment, they would continue their journey tomorrow.

Standing there, amazed by this profound experience, tears streaming down my face, I felt a surge of love enveloping me. Suddenly, a crack and flash pulled me back into the restaurant, gasping for breath, just as Jessie and Harrison walked in.

We exchanged greetings, and Jessie launched into his

story before I could share what had happened. He dreamed of finding himself on the wagon train, choosing to rest at Independence Rock. He witnessed Peter walking toward the rock, which he said was also called the Register of the Desert. Jessie hadn't given it much thought, as it was merely a dream. Yet, he noticed a nearby light and decided to investigate.

When he arrived, he realized that the light was emanating from me. I was glowing, attentively listening to Peter. However, his cat intervened, pouncing on him and abruptly pulling him out of the dream. Jessie described it as a bewildering vision, and as I looked at him with a smile, he asked me why. To the best of my recollection, I recounted everything I had witnessed while Harrison recorded our conversation. Jessie and Harrison sat back in silence as if time stood still. Eventually, Harrison broke the silence, looking at Jessie and declaring the significance. Jessie concurred, acknowledging the unimaginable nature of the shared vision. He explained that he had never heard of two separate individuals experiencing the same vision simultaneously. This realization hinted that time might not be as linear as it seems and that these visions are connected in a timeless realm. Jessie leaned back, admitting that this mind-blowing revelation would require further contemplation and research.

Overwhelmed by what had transpired, we decided to

7 – The Depth of Grief

forgo further work for the day and spend time together. Thus, we spent the remainder of the afternoon engaged in conversation. As the day ended, we said goodbye, promising to reconvene next time. However, I sense that things will never be the same again.

The Understanding
By Mike Russell

When you search your whole life
and know that there is something
that you are reaching out for,
but cannot name.

When your emotions tell you to look harder,
but the passion to find the answer
is always fleeting.

You know that there is something there
but grasping for it, always pushes it away
until you wonder if it got lost in your sanity.

You can look for grief in all the wrong places.
The understanding comes when you realize that you can't escape it.
You can only realize that it has come to you before
and will come again when the time is right.

8 – Destinies Fork in The Road

The Blind Man And The Elephant

It was six men of Indostan, to learning much inclined, who went to see the elephant (Though all of them were blind), that each by observation, might satisfy his mind.

The first approached the elephant, and, happening to fall, against his broad and sturdy side, at once began to bawl: "God bless me! but the elephant, is nothing but a wall!"

The second feeling of the tusk, cried: "Ho! what have we here, so very round and smooth and sharp? To me tis mighty clear, this wonder of an elephant, is very like a spear!"

The third approached the animal, and, happening to take, the squirming trunk within his hands, "I see," quoth he, the elephant is very like a snake!"

The fourth reached out his eager hand, and felt about the knee: "What most this wondrous beast is like, is mighty plain," quoth he; "Tis clear enough the elephant is very like a tree.

The fifth, who chanced to touch the ear, Said; "E'en the blindest man can tell what this resembles most; Deny the fact who can, This marvel of an elephant, is very like a fan!"

The sixth no sooner had begun, about the beast to grope, than, seizing on the swinging tail, that fell within his scope, "I see," quoth he, "the elephant is very like a rope!"

And so these men of Indostan, disputed loud and long, each in his own opinion, exceeding stiff and strong, Though each was partly in the right, and all were in the wrong!

8 – Destinies Fork in The Road

So, oft in theologic wars, the disputants, I ween, tread on in utter ignorance, of what each other mean, and prate about the elephant, not one of them has seen!

John Godfrey Saxe

I should be getting used to leaving the restaurant in a flash, but between the suddenness of movement and the vague sounds of what I can only describe as buzzing, I find myself again at the Wagon Train, which seems to be going nowhere. Still, they are all lined up in a row behind each other. I glance at the back of the Wagon Train and swear that I see Jessie, but he disappears behind one of the wagons just as fast as I think it is him. The Wagons all seem to be without drivers, so I look around and see the men assembled at the front of the Wagon Train. So, that is where I go. Besides, no one can see me, so they won't mind if I join them.

Walking up to the front, I hear someone yell for George Donner, and I see someone ambling to the assembled men. I look down and see the dog, Alder. He stared at me, and we were both confused. I did not think I could be seen. He follows me as I make my way up to George Donner, who is pulling out a letter. He said he was first given a message at Fort Laramie by James Clyman, a mountaineer traveling East with Lansford Hastings. George knew that Hastings was where the Hastings Cutoff had gotten its name. The route was supposed to save them about 400 miles off the regular route. Of course, it sounded good to the Donner group because they knew they were behind schedule, and it would be nice to make up three weeks of traveling.

When they were at Fort Laramie, James Clyman warned the Donners they should not take the Hastings cutoff because he had just come that way, and it would be difficult considering they were traveling in wagons. George Donner thanked him for his information, but Clyman could tell he was determined to make up for lost time.

A second letter was received from a rider heading East when they stopped at Independence Rock. It was written by Hastings urging all emigrants now on the road to meet him at Fort Bridger so he could guide them on his cutoff. George Donner was filling in all the men on the two messages. He told them they had elected him leader of the group, and Donner decided that the best course of action was heading south to Fort Bridger as the new Donner Company that included the Donners and Reeds. They all looked West and could see two distinct trails before them. George Donner stated that this was called The Parting of The Ways and let everyone know that this was the time to say goodbye to the friends that they had made on the trail.

Jed Compton, who hitched a ride with the Keys group at Fort Laramie under questionable circumstances, stepped up in front of the group, saying he knew this route and would like them to hire him as the guide. His only request, other than being able to be part of the group, was to have a horse to ride so he could scout the trail. I, of course, yelled, "NO," but the only one to react was Alder. I remembered being just a viewer, but knowing what happened later to the Donner party made me feel inept. I was happy the Keys party would take the right fork in the road and head further into the Oregon Territory. Donner told everyone to say their goodbyes, so the group dispersed to return to their wagons. On the way, there was a lot of hugging, crying, and shaking hands. Looking down, Alder looked at me as if to ask, now what? I turned and followed the Keys back to their wagons. I felt sad for these folks because their new friendships would end without seeing each other again. I heard Peter Keys tell everyone to get ready to move out, and with that, there was a definite change in behavior as they all moved quicker to ready themselves. Their trail would head them towards the Sublette cutoff and Fort Hall, which would have its trials. But for now, it looked like all was ready, so the wagons were separated into two lines. One would go North, and one would go South.

Flash, I left and was back in the restaurant and, as usual, feeling a little dizzy and nauseous. I thought to myself how decisions made along the trail, although seemingly trivial, could turn into a fight for life, and maybe not knowing what was ahead was the only way these travelers could keep moving forward by using determination and their naïve understanding. In a way, it seemed appropriate because they could deal spontaneously with whatever circumstances arose at any point in time. Looking ahead to different possibilities was not always helpful as it would increase fear. But my heart went to them as they made decisions that day and went into their future stories. I had to rest as I felt drained. I would let Jessie and Harrison know what happened when I saw them next.

Jessie and Harrison were talking as they entered the restaurant days later, and I could tell Harrison had a stunned look. They sat down as usual, and Jessie immediately went into an explanation as I sat down with them. He said he minded his business a few days ago and was suddenly at the Wagon Train. Jessie was confused and dizzy with other feelings but felt that somehow, he was transported to scenes involving my movements within the Wagon Train. He said he was standing at the back of the Keys wagon, looking toward the front of the train, and thought he saw me down there with a group of men. The funny part to him was seeing Alder looking up at me, and the thought crossed his mind that the animal could sense my presence. He felt an awkward feeling of electricity and found himself back where he started, only slightly weaker. That allowed me to fill them in on what transpired since my last visit.

I explained how I had walked up to the front, realized the dog knew I was there, and listened to Donner explain what they were about to do. I also told them how disappointed I was that the Donner party had agreed to let Jed Compton assume the guide duties and gave him a horse as part of the deal. I knew deep down that Jed would add to the drama of the Donner party and felt sad that I could not warn them. After sharing the episode with Jessie and Harrison, we all sat back and relaxed to understand the ramifications. After all, when I spontaneously travel, I can take a sidekick for at least a short time. I could tell Jessie was fascinated but, at the same time, bewildered as we went through the possibilities. Jessie was saying that he had never heard of this before in all his years of research but was open-minded to at least consider the explanation for such a thing happening. He guessed our energies are somehow connected because we have developed a strong relationship. Our energy fields communicate because we are creating a book on this. It sounds impossible, but at the same time, we all agreed that we should be aware of this possibility in case it happens again, and we can document it in more detail. Not knowing if it was a fluke or if it would ever happen again, we put it on the back burner for later and decided to focus on the next adventure.

9 – The Trail Markers to Fort Hall

When we arrived at Fort Hall, we found about 500 Indians of the Flathead tribe who had come to trade. They had buffalo hides and deer skins and would pay any price for beads and tobacco. We bought some buffalo robes and I bought a horse for five pounds of tobacco and a pound of beads. I afterwards sold this horse to the Government for 50.00. We found this tribe of Indians very friendly.

      David Campbell - 1846

I closed my eyes and decided to relax at the thought of going to the Wagon Train during hardship. Opening my eyes, I found I was riding in the wagon next to Peter Keys. He was talking to his family, who were walking alongside the wagon. He said they would take the Sublette Cutoff as he was told it would save fifty miles. The problem, he said, was that there would be no water or supplies on this stretch of the trail. They looked at him and slowly agreed it would be worth the risk to save that much time. I always wondered what it would be like to ride in a wagon, and now I knew. It was bumpy and uncomfortable, and I understood why almost everyone walked. But I stayed with him and saw why this cutoff had a negative reputation. It seemed like there was a dead animal every few yards, which continued for miles. The pull to get to the West was so powerful that they had become numb to the trials of the route and just accepted what was. They were so far from their starting point and had seen so much already that the numbness was second nature. I was tired of riding and went to get off the wagon. Considering we were moving, I realized I did not know how to do that. But the moment I thought that, I jumped into another scene.

Men were tasting the spring water and said it tasted like beer, which I imagine would be a great diversion. Women were excitedly washing their clothes and were talking about Soda Springs as a great place to rest, clean, and recuperate. The kids were swimming along with Alder, the dog. All were having a welcome respite from the trail.

One of the women was making bread using the water from the spring. She was saying it makes the bread light and takes no yeast. She was yelling at the children not to drink the water as they had all noticed that drinking too much of the water was making them sick. This group had been here at the spring for a couple of days, and they all appeared relaxed. I overheard another conversation that they would leave early to head towards Fort Hall. Of course, as soon as Fort Hall was mentioned, I stood before a Fort.

It seemed small and made of adobe, but there was a lot of activity around the fort as it looked like the Wagon Train was stocking up on what they could afford. These folks did not have much money to spend at this point in the journey. Not only was everything priced high, but the choice of items also needed to be improved. So, they did the best they could with what they had. I found the Keys group and saw Peter and Grace talking. They acted comfortably around each other, which made me feel good. They were talking about what was coming up on the journey. They knew they had to cross rivers, mountains, and valleys and still had a long way to go. They talked about how much they missed Sarah and the baby, and Peter, thinking out loud, said he hoped she was proud of them. Grace said she knew her sister was watching over them. Grace felt her presence sometimes. It did not scare her but made her feel like she could make it to Oregon City and help set up a family homestead. She said to Peter that she felt comforted, and although Peter would never admit it, he too felt a presence sometimes. It made me laugh, and for some reason, I got goosebumps all over, and then flash, I was back at the restaurant. I would explain everything to Jessie and Harrison the next time I saw them. What I needed now was rest, as I was completely drained.

10 – The Hidden Secrets in Water

And I would say here a word about traveling and tell it to all of your friends that think of coming on this vast prairie, it is this, do not, as you value your lives, ever drink water out of springs and sunken wells on the side of the road or anywhere else. Always use the Platte River water and you will have no sickness. Even if you do have to go a mile or two miles, do it rather than to drink out of those cursed pitholes of deaths. For it is nothing less than that caused all of our sickness.

We didn't know anything about it, and as the water is generally good and pleasant to drink, we thought we were using the best water. So remember this, and as I said before, advise your friends to do the same. I have not time to write more at present, for we are stopping our teams in the middle of the road for the purpose of writing this. So goodbye for the present. I will write to you again the next opportunity and believe me yours as ever.

George Kiser

While waiting to have another meeting with Jessie and Harrison, I decided to think about everything that had happened so far in my visits to determine if there were parts of the story that I hadn't relayed to them. I realized that I had not talked about the whole of the Keys party, which consisted of two main groups: the Keys and the Leeds. As far as I could tell, both groups combined to be twenty people.

The Keys group included:

Peter Keys

Grace Ames - sister of the deceased Sarah

Aunt Josie Keys - sister of Peter's father

James and Lizzie Travis - son-in-law and daughter to Aunt Josie

Micah and Danielle Travis - son and daughter of James and Lizzie Travis

Aunt Elizabeth Bloom and her husband Thomas Bloom - Aunt Elizabeth was also Peter's father's sister.

Betty, Robert, Devon, and Jo were Thomas and Elizabeth Bloom's children.

Then there are the Leeds group:

Jeremy and Franny Leeds

William Thomas - Franny's father

Michael Leeds - Jeremy's nephew

Penny, Kenneth, and Fran, Children of Jeremy and Franny.

Of course, the group had started with two more, but due to the deaths of Sarah and Adelaide, their combined groups were shrinking. To me, it is incredible that so far, they have only lost two of their group because my understanding is that a good ten percent of the immigrants died for one reason or another on the trail. If the rest of them get to the end of the Oregon trail in one piece, that will be a miracle. So far, I have created this list by being around the families and listening to the different conversations. There could be more I do not know about, but this will help Jessie and Harrison when I meet them next.

I was trying to think of other things that I could convey to them, and of course, I flashed to the inside of the wagon of the Keys. The scene was frantic, and after adjusting, I realized that Peter was lying stretched out on the one so-called bed inside. He was sweating profusely, and I was alarmed to see that his condition was upsetting the rest of the family. Grace and a few other women were desperately trying to bring his temperature down with wet strips of cloth. The smells were horrendous, so I could tell Peter was ill with throwing up and having the runs. He was gripping his stomach in total pain, and I felt so helpless just watching the events unfold. Grace called out to Michael Leeds to get on a horse and ride over to the next wagon train a short distance away to see if he could get the one doctor available in their Wagon Train. They said having a Doctor on any Wagon Train was rare, and although they did not know if it would help, it was worth going and getting him.

Within a short period, there was a commotion outside the wagon, and the head of a youngish man popped into the back of the wagon. He introduced himself as Dr. Garrett Clement and asked everyone to step out of the wagon so he could look at the patient. He stepped in and immediately ascertained that Peter was probably suffering from Cholera, which he knew was one of the scourges of the trip West. He knew that Peter would likely die if he did not do something quickly. Standing outside the wagon, Dr. Clement was talking to Grace and asked her to quickly boil a pot of water so it could cool down. He explained that he needed to get this water into Peter to help cleanse his inside. Dr. Clement knew it would be challenging, but it had to be done. He would also give Peter some liquid from a bottle that he told Grace would help with the pain. The water was boiled and cooled, and he helped Peter sit up and sip some of the water slowly while Grace and Penny applied strips of material soaked in the cool water to Peter's body to bring his temperature down. Dr. Clement told both that it did not matter which disease this was, as quite a few could cause these symptoms. The goal was to get the temperature down and slow the internal distress over the next few hours, as this was the crucial period. If they were victorious by the end of the day, they would either save Peter, or he would die within 24 hours. If they could help Peter survive during that time, he would likely survive, although it would take another 5-7 days to run its course entirely. Both Grace and Penny said they would stay by his side, continue to offer sips of clean water, and keep changing his strips of cloth.

Dr. Clement stayed with Peter for the next few hours, giving advice and letting the rest of the group know that they needed to create a camp for at least a few days. He asked the whole group if there was a well or spring close by from which Peter had possibly drunk. Someone said that he and Peter had been looking for food the day before and had come across a spring. Peter was the only one who had drunk from the spring.

Dr. Clement told the person to return to the spring and

leave a sign stating that the water was tainted so everyone else would know not to drink from it.

He told everyone else that from now on, no one should drink from any water source without boiling the water first. As a new doctor, he explained that the latest training back East included the most updated information on the unhealthy things in water. He said that boiling appears to kill the unknown things in the water. More and more information were coming from other European research, and the findings were that boiling water was best for health.

Everyone on the Wagon Train took his advice, immediately started boiling water, and said they would do so for the rest of the journey. And so, the vigil continued. I chose to stay around and watch over this little group trying to save Peter as I felt so connected.

The women took turns sitting with Peter and changing the strips of linen while Dr. Clement came back every few hours to check on his status. Penny, who was about the same age as Dr. Clement, took a genuine interest in him, and I could tell that something was brewing between them. However, everyone currently focuses on saving Peter and seeing him improve.

By the end of the day, Peter was not getting worse, and his fever seemed to go down. He opened his eyes at one point

10 – The Hidden Secrets in Water

and asked Grace what happened. She explained to him that his sickness was from the water drank out of the spring and that there had been an all-out effort by her, Penny, and Dr. Clement to help get him through the crises. He said to thank everyone and closed his eyes to sleep.

The following day, I found Peter sitting up and drinking water as well as taking another dose of pain meds from the doctor. I felt so relieved to see that he was improving, and as I watched Penny and the doctor walk off together, followed by Alder, I knew that Peter would be okay. The Wagon Train would lose a few days on the trail, but all learned a precious lesson about the dangers of water along the trail. They also realized how lucky they were to have a doctor who understood the new methods of treating different diseases.

In the background, I heard Jessie calling my name and slowly let go of the scene to go back.

Understanding Time

GATHERING BUFFALO CHIPS.

One thing was for sure. The pioneers needed to leave Independence, Missouri, or another jumping-off point in the Spring when the mud issues were low, and the grasses were high to feed the stock. Then, they had to get over the Rocky Mountains before the snow.

So, controlled by these two hard and fast time frames, they had to break down their days into repetitive to-do lists, so to speak, creating a daily routine that not only took care of moving forward but also taking care of all the chores, hunting, repairing wagons, feeding the people and animals, and, oh yeah, sleeping.

I am sure that not all wagon trains were equal because they

10 – The Hidden Secrets in Water

all had different guides, and many people created many voices, but for the most part, they all had to develop a plan of action of when they would do all that was required daily to get to the West in one piece. That is where schedules came in. Taken from many journals and recommendations from those who had gone before them, an average of daily time frames can be laid out, which shows the regimentation.

Begin every day around three a.m. to feed the cattle.

Four a.m.: Sentinels wake everyone up, usually by discharging their rifles. Signals to prepare for the day include bringing in the animals from pastures around the camp.

Six a.m.: Breakfast. Wagons are loaded, and the teams are hitched to the wagons.

A pilot or guide would sound an alarm to move out, usually with a bugle, so that everyone could hear it over the camp's hustle and bustle.

Noon: The pilot and others would ride ahead of the main wagon train to scout a place to rest and eat for an hour until the day's heat dropped.

One p.m.: Wagon Train would be off again until sometime around sundown, where they would once again settle into a camp scouted out ahead of time.

Of course, these time frames were highly subject to the reality of the trail, with its rivers, the need for rafts, and the need to scale hills and mountains by winching the wagons. Every day was a new source of risk and different trials. So, even though they had a schedule, the schedule was a moving target.

Eight p.m.: Once the camp was set up, guards would be stationed around the perimeter for protection. Dinner would come next.

Stopping for the day would allow injuries or illnesses to be addressed, and socializing could occur. Relaxing with hobbies, music, dancing, and camp crafts happened during this time. Eventually, the noise would fade out, and sleep would take over.

This schedule continued day after day, week after week, until they hopefully made it to the West approximately four months later. Adding all the other risk-oriented factors into the puzzle makes one think this journey was utterly crazy. Fortunately, most pioneers did not know what lay ahead, so they just plodded on until they reached where they wanted to go.

Throughout history, this has been the way most migrations occur. It was amazing that the death count wasn't even higher, considering what they had to go through. When occupied by these champions of stress, the West is all the better for it. They settled, farmed, built commerce and cities, and brought the indomitable strength and fortitude to expand the country.

11 – The Union of Minds

I would make a brave effort to be cheerful and patient until the camp work was done. Then starting out ahead of the team and my men folks, when I thought I had gone beyond hearing distance, I would throw myself down on the unfriendly desert and give way like a child to sobs and tears, wishing myself back home with my friends and chiding myself for consenting to take this wild goose chase.

Lavina Porter

Grace Ames was talking to a group of women sitting around a campfire, and of course, I swooped in from the comfort of my restaurant, realizing that I was witnessing a group of women from the Keys and Leeds party.

Grace was talking to Franny Leeds, who a moment before had said that she did not think she could go on. Grace was trying to comfort Franny and let her know she had the strength to make it to Oregon City. Franny went into a discourse about how hard it is to be a woman on the Oregon Trail. We walk all day from sunup to sundown and then must do all the other chores to keep the camp going: cooking, washing, mending clothes, caring for the children, and so much more. I made butter this morning after milking the one cow we have and covering and hanging the bucket under the wagon so it could churn during the day and give us some butter at dinner. There was agreement among the women present. They all looked tired, and I could tell they all realized how much more there was to bear because they were only about two-thirds the way there. Franny said that she is exhausted from the everyday demands of the monotonous trip and the demands of her husband and children. She is afraid of getting sick, like some friends or one of the children getting hurt, let alone the strain on her marriage. Some other women spoke up and said they felt these things as well. Grace said yes, it is hard, and there are times when she feels like she is just going through the motions of moving forward every day. Obviously, this group was being pushed way beyond their everyday routines from back on the farms they came from.

Grace said that she keeps the vision of settling in Oregon as a way of coping and looks forward to the day they can be

11 – The Union of Minds

established on a farm. She spoke to the group compassionately and suggested that they form a women's group that primarily encourages each other and shares in the chores while simultaneously sharing in the work results. For instance, one person could do the butter and share the results, another could be responsible for making bread to share, and others could share in washing dishes and clothes. The children could be responsible for gathering and boiling water for the group. Everyone could share a piece of the hardships with everyone else, so the burden does not crush one person.

They could also all be responsible for helping each other deal with the trials of the mind, which can significantly impact keeping anyone from losing faith in this journey. She asked what the group's opinions were, and there was much discussion around the campfire. But the consensus was that this would provide everyone with great relief, knowing they did not have to suffer alone and could rely on their family and friends. With that, bread was passed around along with Franny's newly churned butter, much to the excitement of everyone. They would inform the men of their joint project and begin right away. Franny told everyone she felt a renewed energy and looked forward to changing her thoughts as she knew her husband and children were counting on her. She, too, looked forward to settling somewhere in Oregon and knew that the future looked hopeful. She thanked Grace for brightening her up and told everyone how much she cared for them.

I watched these women exchange hugs and head to their respective wagons with pride, and I was descended from the blood of this fine stock of women who gave up everything to reach a future of hope. Their hard work and the trials of the trail were something I could only imagine, but somehow, it felt so real and, with that, a flash to where I left. I caught my breath and thought there was something so familiar about these women and wondered how it would all end for them. I thought I would find out.

Jessie and Harrison strolled into the restaurant within a few days, and I joined them. I hadn't told them of all the adventures I had been having with the Wagon Train, and before I could fill them in, Jessie apologized that they had not been around for a while and explained that he had been very sick. Describing his symptoms, they reminded him of food poisoning. He was in bed for a good five days and could not figure out why he could not get better. His symptoms ran from a high fever, stomach cramps, nausea, and everything else. He went to the Doctor and had to drink plenty of fluids. He said that he had only recently felt better after those five days, and the odd thing was it was like a light switch. The

11 – The Union of Minds

illness ended abruptly with no lingering symptoms. He looked over at me, and I was smiling, and he asked what was so funny about that story.

I said I knew why he was sick and proceeded to fill the two of them in on the recent visits to the Wagon Train. After I was all done, Jessie said that although he could do without the actual physical reminders of the events, he thinks that because of his skills as a sensitive psychic, taking on other's emotions and sometimes their physical complaints are typical. Jessie thought that because of my strong connection to both the folks in the Wagon Train and him, he feels we keep seeing an energetic connection. Jessie wondered why his senses did not pick up what I saw, which confused him. It was an exciting question that, although he found fascinating, he still needed to grasp but would continue to put thought into it.

In the meantime, he wondered if I would return to the Wagon Train and pick a scene that was not so emotionally charged. I closed my eyes and found I was in an open grass field but at a high elevation. The Wagon Train was in a circle, and it appeared to be at rest. The skies were bright blue, and beautiful white clouds were floating by. Around the grassy fields off in the distance was a forest of pines that went on for miles.

The Wagon Train was close to what looked like a natural spring. All the livestock were out in the fields eating their fill of grass while the children were running around and playing games in the fields. I went to look for Grace and found her sitting and sewing on some pants. She was talking to Peter and saying how relieved she was that they were spending a few days recuperating in this place of fresh air and beauty. He said this was called Emigrant Springs and was a common stopping point for Wagon Trains after leaving Fort Hall, making it through the rivers and valleys, and into the Blue Mountains. Everyone was exhausted from the changes noted on the trail, which included climbing higher into the hills and then dropping into steep valleys that required much strain on the people and the wagons. The scene here on the mountain seemed more tranquil than I had seen previously.

Peter said that they would head out once the animals had eaten their fill, collected water, and collected game.

It would take a lot of work, of course, as they had to go down the mountain and then head toward The Dalles, which at the time was a small settlement on the Columbia River. It seemed that everyone was more relaxed than the last time I saw them, and as I walked around, it looked like the women were in higher spirits and were all doing different chores, which told me that the agreements made previously seemed

11 – The Union of Minds

to be helping with the day-to-day strain of being on the trail. I felt hopeful for this group of travelers. I knew that there were plenty of things that would test them before they got to the end of the Oregon Trail. Still, they finally looked like they had a joint mission in pursuing their dreams of establishing themselves in a new territory that would bring a more fruitful future than where they came from. I could see the determination of what they were doing in their eyes, and it made me smile. With that, I was back with Jessie and Harrison, helping them to understand that I had seen a turning point. We agreed to meet again, and on the way out the door, Jessie turned back and said he hoped that I could keep him out of the literal feelings of having to take on the diseases on the Wagon Train. He smiled as he left. I knew he was kidding, but something told me there was more to this, and I did not understand it. I went about working in the restaurant and looked forward to our next visit.

12 - Trail Romances

All my soul follows you, love encircles you, and I live in being yours.
Robert Browning to his future wife,
Elizabeth Barrett - 1846

Finding myself back on the Wagon Train was becoming less of a concern because it was happening more often without as much of the corresponding physical and mental strains, for which I am very thankful. This time, I was again in the Keys wagon facing the front and watching two people riding on the wagon seat. I realized it was Peter and Grace, but something was not right.

Peter was driving and asking Grace if she was okay. She said she was a little embarrassed and in pain from falling off the wagon and tripping over the tongue as they prepared to leave Emigrant Springs. Grace thanked him for coming and picking her up and taking her to the back of the wagon while someone went and fetched Dr. Garrett Clement to look at her. Grace said that she noticed that when the doctor arrived, Penny was with him, and she was carrying the doctor's bag. Their relationship had been developing. They both agreed that it was a good thing. Grace said the doctor told her she had a bad sprain. It was good news even though it hurt, and she could not walk.

I looked at her leg propped up on the front of the wagon and saw that the doctor had wrapped it well and someone had made some crutches out of a tree. Now, they were rolling down what looked like a long series of grassy hills, which made Grace hold on as best she could while Peter did his best to guide the oxen in a slow descent with his foot on the brake to prevent the build-up of speed. I could tell that Grace and Peter were uncomfortable, as he reached behind the seat and pulled out a bottle of whiskey. He suggested to Grace that this was going to be even more bumpy than usual, and with the pain, she was in that it would be a good idea to take a shot and dull the pain. She looked at him with the look of someone holding their breath, and I could tell that drinking was not something she wanted to do, but the circumstances required her to do something.

So, she took a gulp, swallowed, coughed, and choked back tears; all the while, the wagon was moving downhill and at a surprisingly steep angle. Within a few minutes, I could tell that the alcohol was starting to set in as she became more relaxed and could carry on a conversation. This scene went on for hours, and she would take a shot anytime she needed to bolster herself. They finally came down enough where the ground was flatter, and she relaxed even more. Peter could eventually take his foot off the brake and loosen on the reins. He pulled to a stop so he could genuinely check on Grace. They both took a breath and hoped that the rest of the trip would not be as dramatic, but they also knew that the most challenging part of the journey was to come. Hopefully, Grace's ankle will heal by then.

So, they started again in a more relaxed way and began talking about how they were pleased to see Dr. Garrett and Penny together as they made a lovely couple, and it looked like Penny was stepping into the role of nurse quickly. Peter agreed and had a faraway look in his eyes. Grace noticed and mentioned that being sad about his wife was okay. Peter said it was not that, but he remembered when he and Sarah first got together and decided to start seeing each other. He noticed that Dr. Garrett and Penny had the same look, and it was just bringing back memories. Grace reached over and placed her hand on his, and said she understood.

They looked at each other in a way I had not seen them

do before, and it made me feel warm all over. I think I was seeing something growing, and maybe Sarah's sister would take on a role that was more than caretaking.

The next thing I heard was Peter humming a tune and Grace saying she knew that as "Arkansas Traveler." They both began singing and within a short time, everyone around them picked it up and sang.

Singing on the Oregon Trail helped to displace the monotony of daily travel. It seemed to lift everyone's Spirits, and Grace felt less pain for obvious reasons. In case it was necessary, I wanted to remember the words to the song, so as they kept repeating it, I memorized the song as:

> Oh, once upon a time in Arkansas
> An old man sat in his little cabin door
> And fiddled at a tune that he like to hear
> A jolly old tune that he played by ear.
>
> It was raining hard, but the fiddler didn't care
> He sawed away at the popular air
> Though his rooftop leaked like a waterfall
> That didn't seem to bother the old man at all.
> A traveler was riding by that day
> And stopped to hear him a fiddling away

The cabin was afloat and his feet were wet
But the old man still didn't seem to fret.

So the stranger said Now the way it seems to me
You'd better mend your roof said he
But the old man said as he played away
I couldn't mend it now it's a rainy day.

The traveler replied that's all quite true
But this I think is the thing for you to do
Get busy on a day that is fair and bright
Then patch the old roof till it's good and tight.

But the old man kept on a playing at his reel
And tapped the ground with his leathery heel
Get along, said he for you give me a pain
My cabin never leaks when it doesn't rain.

It was a joy to see everyone having fun, and as I was feeling the pull to leave, I saw Peter reach out to hold Grace's hand. The smiles between them told me that they would be okay together.

The Least of the Expectations
By Mike Russell

Finding love can be so fleeting.
Within the wellspring of life,
there are so many ways to search, feel and give.

When we are looking, we usually cannot find
what the heart seeks,
until we let go of our fears.

When we decide that we don't have time for it,
it says, now you are ready.
Because it was the least of your expectations,
you get what you need,
not what you want.

13 - Whatever it Takes

In a world where there is so much to be done. I felt strongly impressed that there must be something for me to do.

Dorothea Dix

Instead of returning to the restaurant, I found myself walking up a steady incline beside the wagon. To my surprise, Grace was driving the wagon. Coming up alongside the wagon was Peter on a horse, saying it was about time Grace did something helpful. I realized this was in jest as they looked at each other and laughed. Peter said that it was helpful that Grace sprained her ankle, and he taught her to drive so he could go out at times to hunt. After all, their supplies had diminished, so it was important to find food along the way. Grace took to driving just like she did with all the other duties on a wagon train. She was good at it, and Peter realized he and Grace made a good team and looked forward to their continued partnership. Just as he thought that Grace reined in on the leads and put her foot on the brake while excitedly yelling. Peter thought something was wrong, but as he guided his horse to the top of the hill, he realized what Grace was looking at and raving about. There in front of them was Mt. Hood, rising above the valley. Grace was crying and saying it was the most beautiful thing she had ever seen.

Peter could not argue with that. He got off his horse and just stood in silence. I could see why it would affect them so much, as it is a truly remarkable sight. The other wagons joined them, and a growing assemblage of family, friends, and one dog all stood to take in the scene of the valley below. There were trees as far as you could see and one great mountain in the distance. They also knew that this was the first sign that the pamphlets they all read back East weren't exaggerated and that they were nearing the end of their journey. They also knew that the most treacherous part of the journey was soon to follow. They were approximately twenty-five miles from The Dalles, the small settlement on the Columbia River, where they would have to make some hard decisions relating to the rest of the journey to Oregon City. It would still take them a couple of days to get there, so while they wanted to spend much time taking in this scene, they determined they needed to keep moving.

13 – Whatever it Takes

Then, in a flash, I was back in my restaurant, unable to get the emotional view they all shared that day out of my mind. Imagine seeing something for the first time and now understanding that the trip was not in vain. There was a new Country that they would all share.

They all accepted the hardships gracefully to place themselves and their families in a better life. My family chose to do this profound journey to provide themselves with a chance to improve their lives. The whole picture shot through me as if I were understanding it for the first time. Exhausted, I chose to rest and share this with the boys the next time I saw them.

I don't know how long it had been since I had seen Jessie and Harrison, but when they came walking into the restaurant, I was so happy to see them and share the adventures I had been on. I ran over and sat with them and let them know that something significant had happened and that I needed their input to understand it. I told them about when the Wagon Train saw Mt. Hood for the first time and how everyone was so awed by the view. I told them that I had intended to come back and rest, but as soon as I lay down, I went into a different scene.

I was behind the driver but did not immediately realize who it was. There was a boy of about ten next to him. The boy was so excited to be upfront with his father that he couldn't contain himself. As I listened to their conversation, I realized that this was James Travis, the son-in-law of Aunt Josie Keys. The boy is Micah Travis, and he enjoys being on the wagon with his father.

James told Micah they were only about half a day from The Dalles and the Wascopam Mission. Micah asked what that was, and James said it was a Methodist Episcopal mission established along the Columbia River in Indian Country. They came from the East to spread Christianity, hoping to convert people in the area. He said that we could get there and rest a little. Just as he said that I glanced in the boy's direction and saw him leaning out over the right side of the wagon. At the same time, the wagon hit a large rock with such force that the boy lost his balance and started to go over the side of the wagon and down toward the moving wheels. I do not know what came over me, but I instinctively reached out and pushed him. The surprise to me was that I felt his body. But, in the heat of the moment, I found that I had moved him further out, and instead of falling straight down and getting crushed, he landed hard on the ground but was not completely clear of the wagon. His right leg was in the way of the back wheel, and he had fallen so that his leg was resting against the rock that had just caused the bump. When the rear

13 – Whatever it Takes

wagon wheel hit the rock, it bumped up and came down, catching the front of Micah's leg. At that point, the boy was yelling, and James was trying to stop the wagon while all those walking came running. Dr. Garrett was sent for as Micah was picked up and put inside the wagon. He was propped up and made comfortable.

The Doctor examined the leg and commented that he thought it was broken. The Doctor made a splint. Dr. Garrett mentioned that Micah was lucky that he was not killed while looking at James for an answer. James said it was the strangest thing and retold the story that it looked like Micah was pushed out of the way, and he did not understand how it happened. Dr. Garrett said, well, I guess we can chalk it up as someone is watching over this boy. They discussed that they need to get to The Dalles, where they can devise a plan. They made Micah as comfortable as possible in the back of the wagon, and his sister, Danielle, volunteered to ride with him. Dr. Garrett gave Micah some Laudanum for the pain. The Wagon Train started moving again, hoping to get to The Dalles that afternoon.

I was so weak and confused about the event that I stayed in the wagon with Micah and Danielle in a stupor. How could I interfere with an event and create a different outcome? Until now, I knew I was a witness and just viewing the scenes. No one saw me except the dog Alder, and that is the way that I thought it had to be.

I realized that James was talking to his wife, Lizzie, who had climbed onto the seat. She asked him how it happened, and he tried to explain it. He finally said that dangerous things happen in the blink of an eye, and he will always believe that Divine intervention occurred to save their son. He had no other explanation for it, and Lizzie agreed that, based on their faith, it was the only explanation. It was a quiet ride the rest of the way to The Dalles. I could tell their beliefs had been tested, and they were exhausted.

That afternoon, as they pulled into The Dalles, they made their way to the Mission. Stopping there, a man named Alvin Waller stepped out of the main cabin and greeted them. He helped get the boy out of the wagon and showed them a room they could occupy for a while. Dr. Garrett came up alongside the cabin on a horse and told them to keep him quiet and prop the leg on a pillow. He also gave him a little more Laudanum for the pain. He would return a few hours after they set up the camping area for the night. Danielle said she would stay with Micah as the parents left to help set up camp.

I stayed with the Wagon Train, watched them set up camp over the next few hours, and noticed a man riding up to

13 – Whatever it Takes

the Mission. As he dismounted, he walked up to the main cabin of the Mission and was greeted by Waller. I overheard him say welcome, Sam Barlow. Waller sent out a message for all those on the Wagon Train to meet at the cabin in an hour to discuss options for traveling the rest of the way to Oregon City. The message about the upcoming meeting was passed around the camp from person to person.

Alvin Waller ordered the meeting and introduced Sam Barlow to the many attendees. He started by welcoming everyone to the Oregon Territory. He explained that he and his partner Joel Palmer had arrived just like them a year ago, but due to the late arrival of the Wagon Train in The Dalles, they had missed the last transportation down the Columbia River until the Spring. He said they did not accept the option of wintering in the Dalles. Some of them set out to scout possible other options around Mt. Hood. Even though they could make it, it was rough, and he knew a better road needed to be created. Future immigrants needed an option other than going down a dangerous river. He told everyone that just in the last week, there had been deaths on the Columbia River when the barges that they were using overturned. Everyone was concerned, as I could see it on their faces. He continued his story by letting everyone know that when he got to Oregon City, he went to the Oregon Provisional Legislature to request a charter to construct a toll road along the new route. The petition was approved as the newly named Mount Hood Toll Road. He and Palmer partnered with Philip Foster, who owned a farmstead at the other end of the route near Eagle Creek. He said your Wagon Train, if you decide to use this road, will be the first one since the building of the Toll Road. The tolls were five dollars a wagon and ten cents a head for livestock. He was a fine orator and made the road sound like a better option. He was honest that it would be rough in parts and a lot of work, which involved winching the wagons down certain parts of the road. He said until now, there was only one option: going down the Columbia River to Fort Vancouver and then up the Willamette River to Oregon City. This route was more direct because it ended at Oregon City, one hundred and fifty miles away.

Everyone realized that the rest of the trip would take around ten days, depending on the difficulty of the road. Barlow finished his presentation and said that everyone should get together to discuss what they want to do. He left and entered the cabin to talk to Waller. The Wagon Train took a vote that night and decided to go on the Mt. Hood Toll Road.

At that point, Waller and Barlow asked to see James Travis, and they went to the room where Micah and Danielle

13 – Whatever it Takes

were staying. Outside the door, they talked about how the toll road was very rough in parts, and with that and the other dangers they had been discussing, they didn't think it was a good idea to have Micah go along because of his injury. Dr. Garrett walked in at that moment and, after listening to them, agreed that this part of the journey would cause significant pain and discomfort to Micah until his broken leg healed. Lizzie Travis walked in behind the Doctor and burst into tears, saying that she could not leave her son behind. Waller suggested that Micah stay and looked at Dr. Garrett to confirm how long it would take for the boy's leg to heal. The doctor said with care that it would take a couple of months. Lizzie was distraught, but before anyone could add to the conversation, Danielle said she would stay with Micah while he healed. Then someone could come back for them, or they could follow another Wagon Train to Oregon City when the time comes. They could also help the Mission to pay their way. Danielle was determined that this was the best solution, and after a while, everyone agreed. Lizzie was visibly calmer, knowing that their daughter would be there. Danielle hugged their mother and said the family needed her to be on the Wagon Train. She would be required when they got to Oregon City to help search for a home and care for everyone else. Lizzie looked at Danielle and finally smiled, saying she was proud of her daughter for thinking this all out.

James, Lizzie, and Danielle went into the room to discuss this option with Micah. I cannot imagine how hard that conversation would be, knowing that this was where the family would be separated for a while. But I could tell they were all made of solid stock, and all knew this was the best solution.

Micah had tears in his eyes but put on a pioneer brave face, and even though he was ten, he knew everything would be fine.

I took a breath and looked at Jessie and Harrison. They looked like they were listening to a remarkable story with child-like eyes. Jessie spoke and said Oh My God, you are an influential person to be able to push that kid out of the way so he did not die. He said he thinks the veils are thin between the past, present, and future. He said that this proved to him that emotions connect to the ongoing story, making it charged with energy in a way that somehow affected the timeline. Harrison was amazed and just shook his head. Jessie asked Harrison to research this phenomenon to see if he could find any other reference to this kind of energy interaction between the timelines. They agreed that they would meet back here in a week.

14 – Holding onto Faith

The best protection any woman can have…is courage.
Elizabeth Cady Stanton

My injection into the scenes of this Wagon Train could be something that I would come to expect and would not have those side effects of dizziness and confusion. But it depends on what I am doing at the time of transportation and what scene I am racing into. So, this time, I almost stumbled over a rough terrain littered with rocks as I concluded that I was once again walking alongside the wagons next to Lizzie Travis and Grace. Grace had her arm around Lizzie's shoulder, and she was crying silently. She had just left her two children at a Mission with five buildings and The Dalles, which was not much bigger than that.

She felt she was abandoning them in a territory with many possible outcomes. She knew her pioneer attitude would have to come out substantially, so she did not lose her mind. She told Grace that she had to have faith and focus on the thought that both of her children were safe and in good hands at the Mission, and she would see them again in a couple of months. She was strong and even more robust, having come all this way, but deep inside, she was worried.

She also knew that her daughter Danielle was right, and the rest of the family needed her strength to help set up a homestead at the trail's end. Her faith in God was strong, and as she and Grace walked along the trail that day, they shared reassuring words. As the day wore on, the rest of the women in the Wagon Train all came to Lizzie to show their support. They reminded her to remember what seemed like a long time ago when they promised to support each other in hard and trying times and good times. She thanked all her friends, and somewhere along that day's trail, she relaxed and felt that all would work out. She reflected on the last scene of her daughter Danielle standing at the cabin door as they moved out. Danielle said she loved her and would take care of Micah and, most importantly, would see them soon. I could see that her faith had taken a strong foothold in both her body and Spirit, and it would allow her to hold on until they were united. Her husband, James, looked down from the wagon, smiled, and said he was proud of her strength and believed that their destiny in Oregon included their children. She

14 – Holding onto Faith

reached up, took his hand, and squeezed it as a new tear ran down her face. At that point, I was crying, knowing that these fantastic immigrants strongly believed in something better coming to them as they settled in this country.

They did not know the coming ups and downs, but they had an opportunity to improve their lives and expand the country. Wow, it just made me feel so connected to these ancestors of mine. With that, Jessie showed up next to me on the walk. I could see him through a fog as he smiled at me, and then he vanished as I made my journey back.

The next time I met Jessie and Harrison, Jessie said that when he got flashed into a scene on the Wagon Train and saw that he was walking alongside me, he became emotional. He so wanted to stay there with me but couldn't hold on to the energy required of him. Instead, as he knew he was leaving, he smiled at me. I told him that it somehow made me feel like I was not alone.

Jessie asked Harrison if he could research the scene involving Micah being pushed out of harm's way. Harrison said he found stories about how people were able to travel through time and space and left a mark on the story. From his studies, this appeared to be able to happen under extreme emotions and has been documented in various books throughout history. He said he could not find out if, when someone interferes in the past that way, there is some impact on the time and space continuum. But, based on my experience, he wondered whether that does not matter as much as all time and space are somehow related. It gave him a headache, so we chose to move on to the next adventure.

15 - The Realization of What is Coming

"All the emigrants who came by his road have all safely reached the valley," having abandoned only five wagons in the crossing. Based on the tollgate count, Barlow numbered "one-hundred and forty-five wagons, fifteen hundred and fifty-nine head of horses, mules, and horned cattle all together, and one lot of sheep...." Using Joel Palmer's rough estimate of five persons per wagon, this amounted to over 700 men women and children, which was a substantial portion of the entire 1846 Oregon migration of "1100 to 1200 souls."

Sam Barlow

Jessie suggested I join the family again when they reached the Mt. Hood toll road, which we now know as the Barlow Road.

Harrison had been studying the Barlow Road and said that when you read the accounts written during this time, everyone said this stretch was the hardest of their times on the Oregon Trail. The reason is that there were many places where the wagon had to be winched down the hills. Another method was to tie logs to the back of the wagon for weight and control as the log limbs would grind into the ground and slow the descent.

Flashing into another scene had become so commonplace I did not give it much thought. The side effects had become way less complicated. The only precursor was a blurring sensation from when I left the restaurant to when I got to the scene. This time, I was standing in a beautiful valley, looking at what looked like a small trading post. I was hearing what sounded like a conversation in French and immediately got concerned that I might not be in the right place. But, looking around some more, I saw a Wagon Train approaching from a distance and recognized people I knew. So, wandering around, I saw an encampment of local Indians and the activity at the trading post. Other Wagon Trains settled around the valley in various stages of repairs, resting, trading at the post, and, of course, children running around the camps.

My ancestor's Wagon Train was pulling up to the trading post, and I heard Peter talk to one of the traders. The trader, Jacque, said welcome to Tygh Valley and to move into any open area. Peter moved the wagon out, and the rest of the

15 – The Realization of What is Coming

group followed. When they had settled, he and the other men walked over to the Trading post while the women gathered to prepare a meal and celebrate the cessation of riding the last 35 miles from The Dalles. The men talked to Jacque and were filled in on the upcoming journey into the Cascade Mountains, through the forests, up and down the inclines, and then Oregon City. He said it would take the whole Wagon Train to get the wagons down the mountain into the valley below. Each wagon would, at times, have to be emptied and weighted down, probably with a sizeable dragging log and a winch and pulley system. He suggested they lighten their loads as much as possible, restock what supplies they needed from the trading post, and fix any broken wheels. They would need to be focused to get through the next stretch. The road had been cleared by Barlow and the company last year, but it was very rough in places. The men were fascinated by what Jacque said and wanted him to continue.

So, he explained that they would cross the White River many times on the way to Barlow Pass and the dreaded Laurel Hill. Then, if they made it okay down that hill, they would still have to transverse The Devil's Backbone on the way to Foster's Farm. Then, having come that far, they would be relieved to learn that they were close to the end of the

Oregon Trail at Abernathy Green in Oregon City. He said that most emigrants by that time of the year hold up at Abernathy Green for the Winter while they use that as a base and move out into the Willamette Valley for homestead property. He said it all sounds easy, but the rest of the journey will try their wills to the core over the next ten days. There was total silence as the emigrants were in awe of Jacques telling of the trail, and at the same time, I could tell that they were so tired and a little fearful of what lay ahead that they looked stunned. Everyone thanked Jacque for helping them understand the perils and advise them on how to proceed. They all walked out of the post looking a little gloomy, but as they moved to join their families, Peter took a large breath and talked very confidently about how close they were, how far they had come, and how proud he was to know every one of them. He said what was coming up might be challenging, but he knew they would all make it with each other's help. After all, think about what we all must do once we get there and find land that we can settle on. Peter said that this is nothing compared to what it will take to set up a farmstead.

It was like a light going off in everyone's head. They had not even thought of it until now. They all smiled at each other and shook their heads in unison, stood up straighter, and looked like they had their energy restored. They all went back

15 – The Realization of What is Coming

to their wagons with a newfound sense of excitement. Grace met Peter a few feet away and listened to the whole speech. She smiled at him and kissed him on the cheek with the pride of someone who fell in love with this strong man on the trail. I tingled all over and got goosebumps, and I could not help but agree with her. My connection to Peter and the whole extended family was overwhelmingly strong. Right then, I knew their story was my story, which was bigger than I knew. I was thinking about that and found myself back in the restaurant, staring into Jessie's eyes as he was smiling with the same understanding.

Jessie believed that he and I were somehow related through this story.

He sensed the energy involved and our repeated connections throughout the journey. A more extensive narrative was at play, although he hadn't pieced it together entirely. I agreed, acknowledging that something significant was unfolding, and I looked forward to unraveling the mystery alongside Jessie and Harrison. They left, promising to return soon.

16 - Facing the Odds with Determination

They had a good camp and prepared themselves for what would become known as the "ultimate challenge." This was the treacherous Laurel Hill - a declivity "so steep that a year after opening significant erosion had occurred, and by 1852 the ruts were six feet deep. Negotiating this notorious slope required ingenuity. Some slid wagon beds down 60 percent grade or put two yoke of oxen on each end of the wagon. Others rough-locked wheels and/or dragged logs up to 100 feet long. Another option was to snub [repel] wagons around trees with ropes, a process which scarred some trunks badly, and ... possibly broke off 10 to 14-inch [in diameter] trees." Barnet Simpson commented that "none of the emigrants who came down this steep grade with men

pulling on ropes to keep the wagons from running over the oxen, will ever forget Laurel Hill."
Trail Descendant - Ross A Smith

A sense of disorientation overcame me as I stood at the top of the mountain. The steep descent ahead seemed impossible, and I heard the exclamation of shock from behind me. One wagon was in the middle of the treacherous path, its progress hindered by a massive log dragged behind it. Cursing and yelling filled the air as the driver struggled to steer the oxen away from the deep ruts forming beneath the wagons. The danger became evident as the wagon lost control, tipping over and violently throwing off its occupants. The wagon broke apart, and the frightened oxen bolted for the trees while the wagon's contents scattered down the mountain. Panic ensued above and below as people rushed through the trees and down the slope to assist the injured.

I watched as the injured individuals were carried down to a flat bench of land at the bottom of the mountain while others cleared the wreckage off to the sides of the trail. The oxen, now calmer, were also rounded up and brought down. It was a stark reminder that the dangers on the trail were not just stories but harsh realities. The family I had been traveling with stood beside me, referring to this perilous section as

16 – Facing the Odds with Determination

Laurel Hill – the most complex and dangerous part of their Oregon Trail journey. They were rightfully horrified by what they had just witnessed, yet they also displayed a sense of acceptance and determination.

They did their tasks without hesitation, preparing their wagons for the descent. They cut down a tree to use as a brake and secured ropes around sturdy tree trunks to assist in winching the wagons down the hill slowly and safely. They vowed to take the necessary precautions to prevent a repeat of the earlier tragedy. After spending considerable time preparing, the family's oxen and wagon approached the edge, and Peter, taking the lead, guided them down the precipice. The other men held onto the ropes wrapped around tree trunks, trying to avoid the dragging log. The rest of the party watched with bated breath as the wagon descended slowly.

Peter skillfully maneuvered, avoiding the deep crevices carved by previous wagons, knowing the consequences of tipping too far. When he reached the bottom, he yelled triumph before moving the wagon out of the way and ascending the hill to assist with the next wagon.

The family members repeated this process throughout the day, helping each wagon down the mountain. Peter's hands were bloodied from the strain of the reins and the ropes around the tree trunks. But they all wore their wounds of hard work with pride, feeling accomplished by the day's end. They rested in a pasture away from the bottom of Laurel Hill, knowing they were nearing the end of their provisions, and the oxen were nearing exhaustion.

Despite their fatigue, they scavenged for food for themselves and the animals, gathering what little they could find.

With renewed hope, they set their sights on Oregon City, eager to complete their journey.

My heart went to them as I realized it was time to leave. Their trials weighed heavily on me, and I felt sad as I returned to the restaurant. Exhaustion consumed me mentally and physically as if I had lived through the day's challenges alongside them. Another day on the trail would come, and I knew I would be there to witness it. But for now, I needed to rest and recover from the profound energy of their journey.

17 - The Meeting of a Giant

"His benevolent work was confined to no church, sect nor race of men, but was as broad as suffering humanity, never refusing to feed the hungry, clothe the naked, and provide for the sick and toilworn," so spoke Willard H. Rees in 1879 at a meeting of the Oregon Pioneer Association, about Dr. John McLoughin.

Peter gathered several train members and announced, "We made it." Despite being accustomed to my sudden presence in the middle of conversations, it still had a disorienting effect. We found ourselves in a field near a river, finally reaching Oregon City and Abernathy Green. Due to the lateness of the season, they would spend the Winter here and set out in groups over the next few weeks to search for suitable homestead properties.

Peter mentioned his cousin, who had already settled in

the Tualatin Plains. They would help each other find land with access to water, timber, and fertile soil for planting. Excitement filled the air, but exhaustion hung heavy upon everyone, including the weary animals grazing in the pasture.

A murmur rippled through the group as a man approached and introduced himself as Dr. John McLoughlin—his imposing figure, adorned with long white hair, contrasted with his soft Scottish accent. It seemed that most of the people present were familiar with him, but for those who weren't, he explained that he had recently retired as head of Fort Vancouver for the Hudson's Bay Company and had built a home in Oregon City for his family. He acknowledged the hardships endured on the trail and assured them they could now focus on establishing homesteads. Dr. McLoughlin offered assistance during their Winter stay, expressing his willingness to help and share his extensive knowledge of the area to guide them toward good-quality farmland.

Several men immediately requested his advice and gathered around him, engaging in a spirited discussion about their plans. Meanwhile, the rest of the wagon train set up a temporary camp using tents and any available shelter. Dr. McLoughlin mentioned the presence of stores, a sawmill, and other homes in Oregon City.

17 – The Meeting of a Giant

Peter remarked that it was the largest town they had seen in a while, bustling with activity on the land and the river. The group agreed and continued their questions until they were satisfied. Dr. McLoughlin walked away with a farewell and well wishes, leaving those who remained standing transfixed by his commanding yet gentle presence. Peter expressed his belief that Dr. McLoughlin exuded greatness, a sentiment shared by everyone as they dispersed to work on their Winter quarters. I, too, stood there, captiveated by the encounter.

Witnessing Dr. McLoughlin in person added a new perspective to life in this new Northwest country and reinforced the notion that it takes a diverse array of people to make a dream come true. No one person can accomplish it alone. I knew that history would remember Dr. McLoughlin favorably, and his presence reaffirmed my belief in the intricate planning behind the Wagon Train journey and my interaction with my ancestors.

Finding myself back at the restaurant, I yearned to see Jessie and Harrison, unsure when that opportunity would arise. I longed to share the recent adventures and encounters with historical figures, sensing that these experiences were not coincidental but part of a larger plan beyond my comprehension. I spent the remainder of the day attempting to piece together the puzzle and formulate a coherent explanation to share with them during our next meeting.

A few days later, I finally saw the two individuals who had become dear to me. Jessie's focused gaze as I relayed the stories made me blush, but I was determined to continue. Harrison asked numerous questions, and we spent a couple of hours conversing, taking notes, and addressing their inquiries. Eventually, I realized my responsibilities at the restaurant and excused myself, leaving them engaged in conversations.

As Jessie and Harrison prepared to leave, Jessie suggested that our next adventure should involve visiting where the family eventually settled and established a homestead. I wholeheartedly agreed, expressing my anticipation of seeing them soon. I watched as Jessie walked out the door, but before he disappeared, he turned around, locked eyes with me, and smiled, accompanied by a nod of acknowledgment.

18 – Out of the Darkness

The footsteps of a pioneer become ultimately the highway of a nation.

Ameen Rihani

The voice of Jessie gently encouraging me to visit the wintering camp at Abernathy Green in Oregon City brought me to a festive scene of everyone surrounding a large fire. The stars were out with a noticeably clear sky, providing a view of a group of people that I almost did not recognize. They all looked rested and well-fed. I saw a feast of salmon, berries, and other crops. Peter was telling someone that the arrival of the Wagon Train was at a fortunate time of the year when the bounty of fish and crops was plentiful, and they had been able to restore themselves and the animals during the last month. In addition, Peter was delighted over a piece of land he had filed a claim on with the government land office in the Tualatin Plains, about 18 miles away. After scouting the area, he and several other families decided to move there as there was plenty of water, wood, and excellent soil. They had been able to resupply their stores at the Abernathy Mercantile and other stores in Oregon City. The plan was to move the wagons and family to the land as soon as the let-up of Winter allowed them to move in that direction. For Wagons, travel is impossible right now due to the wet conditions, which cause mud bogs and impassible areas. As much as they wanted to get there immediately, they knew the right decision was to wait.

Dr. McLoughlin helped some of those on the train get through the Winter because the journey completely drained several of the parties' stores and assets, so much so that some folks barely made it to the so-called promised land. The help was much appreciated, and because of it, the whole Wagon Train would make it through to Spring.

Grace was sitting with Lizzie, whose children were left behind at The Dalles because Micah Travis had a broken leg, and his sister Danielle chose to stay and care for him until he healed.

Lizzie told Grace that the two kids were all she could think about, especially since they made it to Oregon City. She can't help but wonder how they are and if they are safe. Lizzie is trying hard not to be too sad. Grace put her arm around

18 – Out of the Darkness

Lizzie and talked to her reassuringly. She let her know that the kids were in good hands. Grace didn't know for sure but wanted to help her friend through this low period.

As she was saying this, I looked toward the opposite side of the camp, and through the flickering light extended by the large fire, I could see movement in the darkness. Slowly, forms started to move towards us. I could see three people moving out of the shadows of the trees. I couldn't tell who they were yet.

I heard Lizzie say that she just wanted to hug her kids, and a voice came from the three forms approaching that "it might be able to be arranged." All those present turned towards the voice, and Lizzie screamed. She ran over to the forms, yelling until she met her children, who could now be seen in the firelight. Tears flowing and people crying and screaming while jumping up and down created quite the vision. I was even crying as I heard Micah say that his leg healed. He said Alvin Waller needed to go to the valley for a meeting and was going to ride a horse there. Then Alvin wondered if we would like to join him. He noticed that his leg had healed nicely, and he thought that we could all make it to Oregon City and catch up to you. Thankful handshakes were extended to Mr. Waller, and everyone was directed back to the fire, where food was to be shared. The relief on Lizzie and

James Travis's faces was priceless. They had their family back together and could progress to their claim together. It looked like Alder, the dog, even knew what was happening as he ran around in circles and greeted the three as jubilantly as everyone else. Mr. Waller asked if some food might be available as it was limited to what they brought. All the women jumped into action, and as I started to depart, I could see Lizzie not wanting to let go of her kids. It reminded me that time doesn't matter regarding family and their love for each other.

When I returned, I asked Jessie if he felt he and I connected through this story. He said, of course, that it would be revealed in time. I now think there is a reason I can travel on these adventures. There must be a connection to some shared storyline that involves all of us. My understanding of Karma and past lives is extremely limited to conversations I picked up over the years in the restaurant, but there seems to be a connection. As Jessie says, I hope all will be revealed by the time this story ends. Jessie suggested that the natural next step would be joining the family after they had set up their homestead. It might reveal the results of all their struggles. I agreed to that, but after that, I could rest for a while. We decided to meet the following week to have the adventure that could be the last.

Against All Odds
By Mike Russell

Looking through the clouded tears,
trying to comprehend the significance.
Understanding that the lack of belief
is only seen from one side.

Coming out of the darkness
takes courage and determination.
Believing that there is impact
that one can have on their world,
strikes a balance between fear and belief.

Never knowing how you got where you are,
but for the charity of your own internal guidance,
will give you the strength to challenge
the confines of the darkness.

19 - The Future is Understood

Still round the corner, there may wait, a new road or a secret gate.

J.R.R. Tolkien

"Dearly beloved" was the first thing I heard as I came out of the fog of time travel. I realized that I was standing behind a wedding ceremony inside a cabin. The exciting thing is that four people were at the front with a room. The room was full of men, women, dogs, and cats. They were all standing around listening to a minister I recognized as Mr. Waller. I glanced to my right and saw Jessie standing beside me, smiling in my direction. That alone threw me for a loop, but I decided to focus on who was getting married. I realized that the double wedding consisted of Peter and Grace, Dr. Garrett Clement, and Penny Leeds. My heart melted as I realized that I was seeing the continuation of the family.

We were also standing in a newly completed cabin.

These budding romances had to wait until construction was done. This was the first time this event could occur. Reverend Waller said he was pleased to be here on this special occasion and welcomed the opportunity to marry the fine young people he had known. He relayed the stories of how both couples had come to meet on the Oregon Trail and asked if there was any reason why these couples should not be married.

Jessie somehow reached over to touch me, and although we did not have physical bodies, I did feel a strong jolt of energy run through me as we energetically touched hands. We smiled at each other, and both understood the importance of these two marriages to the future of the families in the Oregon Territory.

Peter took the opportunity to speak up and say a few words about Sarah and Adelaide Keys. He said that although they didn't make it with them to Oregon, they were there the whole time in Spirit, helping them along the way. Sarah was a strong woman when they left and was excited about the future, but she and the baby left them too early due to unfortunate circumstances. He started to get choked up, so Grace stepped in and continued. She said my sister was beyond any friend I could have. Sarah loved me without exception and was always a role model to me. When Adelaide

19 – The Future is Understood

was born, I saw her embrace that little being with all the love she had, and when the baby died so tragically, I saw her very quickly fold into herself with grief, which resulted in her death. But I want to remember her and the baby in the loving way she showed everyone on the Wagon Train. I want her memory to represent all those who came across and fought the hardness of the trail with strength and determination, no matter what the outcome was.

Please take a moment to remember those who did not make it and gave us all the strength to carry on.

Of course, I was shaking, and tears were rolling down my face as I glanced at Jessie and reached for him. The energy of the two of us swirled together and flashed many pictures of lifetimes together, making me realize that our time spent together was part of a much bigger plan. As the scenes flew by, we both ended up at the Wagon Train and the repeated scene of the death of Sarah Keys. She was down by the water after the baby had died. Our combined energies were standing by her, and through her distraught nature, she was talking out loud as if in a prayer. She said that she knew she was being heard, and even though her journey would still be over, she wanted to connect with the understanding that it would all be okay because the future is secure. She said Sarah out loud, and I jumped because I felt she knew I was there, which did not make sense. She said she had a dream before this all happened and knew that she would continue with the family even though it would not be physical. Sarah hoped that Sarah, in the future, could forgive her once the true nature of the whole story was realized. She said that even though she would not be seen, Peter would always be there for her, and they would work together in the future. She said love continues no matter what happens in the present, and with that, she turned her head and looked directly at us.

She smiled with great radiance even though tears were streaming, made a forward gesture with her body, and slipped into the water. I screamed and immediately felt the movement into many more lifetimes as we saw scene after scene throughout the progression of time until the movement stopped with a jerk. I was standing at the top of the stairs in the restaurant, and Jessie was standing at the bottom, looking up at me. In that instance, I understood everything. I never realized it on the Wagon Train, but I looked exactly like Sarah then. As a sudden understanding, my focus was on Jessie, who I knew was Peter, and all the other characters throughout our stories together. I knew that I was Sarah then and now, and she was telling me it would be okay. I looked down at my body and saw that I was floating. I could see that I was wispy in appearance. So, this is what she meant about forgiveness. I was Sarah, and I am a Spirit. Jessie reached out his hand, which I took as we headed toward Harrison's table.

Before you say anything, Jessie said he was recently able to put the story together based on his dreams and clairvoyance. He knew that he had been drawn here to this place for a reason. But until today, I have not been able to put it all together. He knows now that he was Peter in that lifetime and that we have been together many times throughout history. The only difference now is that I did not move on from that last lifetime, and he did. He said that everything flooded in when we touched hands at the wedding, especially after they found Sarah by the river. She had insight as well and knew what was going to happen. She also knew we would be together again, which is why this had all transpired.

20 - Stepping Into The Unknown

You venture into the unknown land because that is where your heart will take you. In the end, it is not what you want to do, it is something you have to do.
Laura Ingalls Wilder

As the truth of our intertwined journeys unfolded, and the realization that I had been a Spirit all along settled with me, I made a firm declaration to Jessie and Harrison: I wasn't going anywhere. As Jessie suggested, departing into the light did not resonate with me. I had taken a long time to reunite with Jessie, in whatever form it may be, and I had no intention of leaving him again, at least not until his own time to depart arrived. Until then, I wanted to stay by his side, and what I desired most was to embark on new projects with Jessie and Harrison.

This unique situation of being a spirit while Jessie and Harrison worked together presented an extraordinary opportunity for us to form a team that could positively impact many lives. It was a chance to make a difference and create a life I could be proud of while being with the person who intricately woven our stories. I had come to understand the profound significance of Jessie in my life, both in the past and present, and I yearned for our connection to continue.

As I expressed my plans, Jessie and Harrison sat in stunned silence. As the intermediary between Harrison and me, Jessie conveyed my words to him, and I now realized that he had been the bridge connecting us all along. Looking back on our conversations, it became clear that Jessie and I communicated directly, with Jessie relaying messages to Harrison. There were many signs and peculiarities throughout our journey that could have hinted at the nature of our relationship. But perhaps it was for the best that the veil of understanding was gradually lifted, protecting me until I was ready to see the bigger picture.

Once the initial shock subsided, Jessie and Harrison recognized the potential of this unique partnership. They agreed to embark on this journey with me, but they acknowledged that adequately telling the story of the Wagon Train would require significant time and effort over the next year. Jessie expressed the happiness that I had chosen to continue with him, as he had been grappling with finding a

20 – Stepping into the Unknown

way to stay together without being selfish by asking me to stay.

I suggested it was time for us to reunite outside the confines of the restaurant. Considering the extended period I had spent in that space, the only uncertainty was what would happen when I attempted to step beyond the threshold. I expressed excitement and a hint of fear, and in response, Jessie invited me to his spacious house. He hoped we could embark on a grand adventure together by creating a foundation for our future and exploring this extraordinary relationship.

With his hand outstretched, I took it, feeling his energy course through me as we approached the door.

As Harrison and Jessie stepped through the door, I gazed at the threshold, taking in the scene of a place that had always been a part of me. Jessie looked back at me, a smile gracing his face, and with that reassurance, I took a step forward into an unknown but thrilling future. I was embarking on a new chapter with the man I had loved through countless lifetimes and in various forms. The creaking door closed behind us, marking the end of a chapter and announcing, at least to me, that life continued to unfold despite the challenges of the Oregon Trail and the sorrow I had experienced within those walls. Our Spirits had an incredible capacity to connect profoundly, given the opportunity.

As we stepped into the unknown, a song echoed in my mind, the lyrics capturing the essence of our journey:

I'll Never Find Another You
By The Seekers

> There's a new world somewhere
> they call the promised land.
> And I'll be there someday
> if you could hold my hand.
> I still need you there beside me
> no matter what I do.
> For I know I'll never find another you.

Lansford W. Hastings
The Emigrants' Guide to Oregon and California - 1846

In view of their increasing population, accumulating wealth, and growing prosperity, I can not but believe, that the time is not distant, when those wild forest, trackless plains, untrodden valleys, and the unbounded ocean, will present one grand scene, of continuous improvements, and unparalleled commers: when those vast forests, shall have disappeared, before the hardy pioneer; those extensive plains, shall abound with innumerable herds, of domestic animals; those fertile valleys, shall groan under the immense weight of their abundant products; when those numerous rivers, shall team with countless steamboats, steamships, ships, barques and brigs; when the entire country, be everywhere intersected, with turnpike roads, railroads and canals; and when, all the vastly numerous and rich resources, of that now, almost unknown region, will be fully advantageously developed. To complete this picture, we may fancy to ourselves, a Boston, a New York, a Philadelphia, and a Baltimore growing up in a day, as it were, both in Oregon and California, crowded with a vast population, and affording all the enjoyments and luxuries, of civilized life. And to this we may add, numerous churches, magnificent edifices, spacious colleges, and stupendous monuments and observatories, all of Grecian architecture, rearing their majestic heads, high in the aerial region, amid those towering pyramids of perpetual snow, looking down upon all the busy, bustling scenes, of tumultuous civilization, amid the eternal verdure of perennial spring. And in fine, we are also led to contemplate the time, as fast approaching, when the supreme darkness of ignorance, superstition, and despotism, which now, so entirely pervade many portions of those remote regions, will have fled forever, before the march of civilization, and the blazing light, of civil and religious liberty; when genuine republicanism, and unsophisticated democracy, shall be reared up, and tower aloft, even upon the now wild shores, of the great Pacific; where they shall forever stand forth, as enduring monuments, to the increasing wisdom of man, and the infinite kindness of protection, of an all-wise, and overruling Providence.

Closing Thoughts of the Future

While the description above of the future, written in 1846, accurately predicted the transformation of the Oregon Territory, it came at a significant cost to all involved. Humans envision progress that may benefit their souls and way of life, often disregarding the consequences for others.

The native cultures suffered immensely from this westward movement, experiencing disease, famine, wars, and the loss of their way of life. The destruction of the buffalo herds and other animals in the path of progress is a testament to the price paid.

Numerous changes had to occur to arrive at the predictive description above. As a nation, we had to suppress all forms of protest and conform to the ideologies controlling our thoughts. Our ancestors were stubborn, righteous, and unyielding. They established treaties that held little meaning and pushed forward, disregarding the consequences of those decisions made long ago.

How can we reflect on and respond to everything that transpired in the name of "manifest destiny?" It is unlikely that the current generations can fully make amends for the mistreatment inflicted upon those who suffered during that time in history. However, history tends to repeat itself. While apologies and forgiveness play a role in healing a nation, understanding the truth and remembering the lessons learned can contribute significantly.

Even now, as the predictions made in the past have come to fruition, similar injustices occur worldwide. The indigenous people of Brazil, with their burning forests, serve as a prime example. Many cases across the globe reflect the same patterns of judgment and discrimination that mirror the actions of our ancestors in the 1800s. Most individuals during that era likely did not perceive their thinking as inherently wrong; it was merely a way of life, and everyone wanted their share of the pie. There is nothing wrong with seeking prosperity, but when a country relies on one-sided narratives to shape its history, many truths can become twisted to serve the interests of a few. Humanity often repeats similar storylines, mistakenly believing they represent new and progressive thinking.

In the future, we can envision a time when all people come together at the same table to discuss what is beneficial for themselves and the collective good. Unlike the broken treaties of the past, let us hope that we can save this planet from ourselves and predict a future free from past mistakes. Being naïve is one of my strong points, but I remain hopeful that our unity will triumph over self-interest.

Mike Russell

I hope that no more groans of wounded men and women will ever go to the ear of the Great Spirit Chief above, and that all people may be one people.

Chief Joseph

About the Author

Mike Russell

In the formative era of the 1950s, Mike Russell's childhood was steeped in the allure of movies and television westerns, igniting his imagination and fostering a deep curiosity about history and humanity's propensity to forget the lessons of the past.

His journey from broadcasting school to journalism and photography cultivated a nuanced understanding of people and a relentless pursuit of existential meaning. Through introspection and a dedicated study of Yoga, he embraced a broader perspective on spirituality, transcending the boundaries of known and unknown realms.

Russell's fifth book delves into his evolving concept of spiritual existence. Preceding works include *A Journey of Discovery through Intuition with Help from the Angels, My Compass, Our Story: A Journey through Death and Life, What's in the Water? Our Soul's Reflection on Spirit and Self,* and *A.R.C. - Archangel Raphael Conversations.*

The passing of his first wife, Barbara, forced him to confront his spiritual values after a thirty-four-year marriage, prompting a soul-searching quest to rediscover his true self. Ultimately, he found solace and renewal through writing, leading to a second marriage to a kindred spirit deeply entrenched in the realm of energy.

Returning to the insatiable curiosity of his youth, Russell found himself inexorably drawn to new adventures and experiences that have fueled his writing ever since. Embracing the moniker of the "Knowledge Seeker," he revels in the exploration of diverse subjects and pledges to continue his literary journey with unwavering passion.

www.ingramcontent.com/pod-product-compliance
Lightning Source LLC
LaVergne TN
LVHW010214070526
838199LV00062B/4586